About the Author

B K Jackson is an author based in the west of Scotland. He is a former artist who took to writing as an alternate creative outlet during the Coronavirus lockdown process in early 2020.

He is an avid suspense and true crime fan. He lives happily in Scotland with his family.

Dear Dan

Remember, the only darkness is in your imagination!

Enjoy

B K Jackson

LORD OF THE DEAD

*Bloody Tales of Nicolas Claux,
the 'Vampire of Paris'*

AUSTIN MACAULEY PUBLISHERS™

LONDON • CAMBRIDGE • NEW YORK • SHARJAH

A CIP catalogue record for this title is available from the British Library.

ISBN 9781528967617 (Paperback)
ISBN 9781528971249 (ePub e-book)

www.austinmacauley.com

First Published 2022
Austin Macauley Publishers Ltd
1 Canada Square
Canary Wharf
London
E14 5AA

Dedication

Kelly, Saya, my dad Keith, my sadly departed mum Lynda, Michelle, Ben and Lucy-fur

CONTENTS

INTRODUCTION

TRUE CRIME STORIES have always been a popular and fascinating genre. In earlier centuries, the public would gorge themselves on one-page broadsheets, typically embellished with woodcuts and doggerel verse and breathlessly relaying news of the latest grisly crime or almost as grisly punishment. Towards the end of the nineteenth century, newspapers started getting in on the act when they realised how many more copies they could sell with a juicy murder on the front page. Soon, full-length books began to be written about the most notorious crimes, increasingly concentrating on the people who committed them. Now, whole television channels are dedicated to true crime documentaries and re-enactments, while the internet has given still greater access to this information and even added formats of its own, such as blogs and podcasts.

A simple enquiry via an online search engine will present the avid researcher with all of the available facts and timelines in a matter of seconds, giving them a wealth of information on their particular chosen subject. Gone are the days in where a person could only get the barest of facts from the tabloid press and news programmes and needed to wade through library microfiches in order to discover the details they had been looking for. These days a person can choose to read through online articles, studies and even interviews and in this way gain a fair understanding of what may have occurred. In theory, they can come to their own conclusions based on what they have learnt from a series of non-biased journalism and interviews.

Or can they?

It has long been my opinion that most forms of newspaper journalism and, to a greater degree, TV documentaries relating to the subject of true crime, have not taken a truly neutral standpoint when recording the facts and opinions of the case. Take the example of the person who could be arguably deemed the world's most notorious modern serial killer, Ted Bundy. In the vast majority of television documentaries that I have watched about Ted Bundy, the story of his crimes has been told from the viewpoint of his surviving victim, the law enforcement officers who were involved in solving his crimes and bringing him to justice, and even, in a way, from the viewpoint of those victims who did not survive, in the guise of interviews with their relatives. The interviews which Ted Bundy himself gave to television channels or other media tend to have been edited to tell the tale so that it would fit in with the documentary's already established viewpoint. The questions that the interviewer asked would be seeking the answers which they wished to have clarified, and would not necessarily have given any insight into what Ted Bundy himself may have wished to discuss, assuming he had been given a full opportunity to do so. In other words, the evidence shown to the vast majority of television viewers, whilst accurate in terms of physical facts, would not be entirely accurate since the perpetrator, in this instance, was not able to tell his side of the story, should he have wished to do so. Even when Ted Bundy's death sentence was carried out, the depiction shown to the watching world was from the viewpoint of law enforcement, as well as whichever way a particular news channel chose to disclose the information at the time.

Ted Bundy is just one example. There are countless others. Of course, I appreciate that not every perpetrator of true crime may wish to tell their story in detail, whether because they think this may lead to further persecution from law enforcement, or even because they wish to hold onto some details of their crimes and their thoughts about them as a means of maintaining a degree of personalisation and uniqueness towards them. We will never know the true motivations of convicted killers like Harold Shipman or even Jeffrey Dahmer as they were never able to give their full accounts of the extent of the details to their crimes before their deaths. So whether intentional or otherwise, the deaths or subsequent execution of particular crime perpetrators have a gaping hole in our information about these individuals, information that may have proved pivotal for an avid researcher of true crime to complete the picture within their own minds, and as a result get a better understanding of the events as a whole.

This situation is not entirely confined to convicted murderers. There are many ways in which the public never get to understand the complete picture of what unfolded prior to the point of capture by law enforcement, and subsequent trial and punishment. One example of this would be the Italian Mafia in the USA: *Cosa Nostra*, 'Our Thing', as it is known by members of the Mafia. There are many reasons why the details of these crimes have not become available to members of the public, in which they could, once again, obtain all of the information from all accounts, and as a result, obtain a better understanding of the crimes. One of the main reasons in this instance is the Mafia's principle of *Omerta*, which is usually translated as a 'code of silence'. Under strict Mafia rules, this, once broken, is punishable by death. Unless a former Mafia member has broken away from the ranks of these particular crime organisations, and exchanged information relating to the organisation in order to obtain a lenient prison term, they seldom reveal information about their crimes. (An example of one such defector from the Mafia is Salvatore 'Sammy the Bull' Gravano.) From what seems to be the consensus on platforms such as YouTube, people have a yearning for the inside and personal stories and accounts of high-ranking Mafia members such as John Gotti, so that they can fill their particular knowledge void, and get as clear an understanding as possible.

It is human nature to want to know (even if we cannot understand it) the fuller details of every crime. When an interested person sits down to watch a documentary or read a true crime book, they do so because they want to try and fathom what they can about the thoughts of the person who carried out the murder or crime. The human mind, whilst not always able to comprehend the physical actions of a murderer, has is a morbid fascination with what they deem to be the unknown, especially in terms of what goes on within the mind of the murderer: what makes them tick, what makes them cross that fine line from fantasising about the crime, to evolving that thought into action. It is that very separation from themselves into what is considered to be taboo that drives the interest in the mind of a true crime researcher or enthusiast.

It has been my experience that, within the vast majority of the stories of true crime being told, this is the one missing element that would make the puzzle complete. There are so many stories that have such an amazing hook-line, drawing in the viewer, but unfortunately they are often left wanting to know more. Whilst I understand that this may be what a great number of people relish, as it leaves the mind open to imagination and mystery, I feel that more can be offered in giving a person the full spectrum of events and thoughts, and giving their imagination more to work with, ticking all of the proverbial boxes.

It is here, with the information missing from so many true crime stories, that we arrive at what makes this book so different. This is a true crime story; the sequence of events is told in chronological order and from an honest perspective. The story is not meant to glamorise the events that unfolded, nor to judge or condemn the actions and events either. It will simply tell the honest tale of a particular criminal, from the early onset of childhood where the foundations of what would later unfold were first built.

This is the story of Nicolas Claux: an account of his life that could be told by none other than the man himself. In this story we will get access into the mind of a man whose actions, for most people, appear wholly impossible to comprehend. This story will give the full and honest account of the details of his life, and how he evolved into the person who would be dubbed by the media 'The Vampire of Paris'.

ONE

BIRTH AND CHILDHOOD

THE CONCEPT OF *Dharma*, cosmic law and order: this is applied to mental constructs or what is recognised by the mind. In some of the ancient translations into English, its meanings could include 'order', 'duty', 'custom' and 'model': all of the elements deemed in a manner to serve the being and avoid creating chaos within the mind, or even within the body of oneself. It is said that one must follow the path which is felt or deemed to be the most natural to the individual. To stray from one's natural actions or behaviours would be considered to be *Adharma*, and as such would be unethical and wrong, and against the nature of the individual, thus causing inner chaos of the mind.

In the late 1960s, Nicolas Claux's father was called up for compulsory National Military Service at the age of 18. This was still in place in France at the time; it would eventually be phased out between 1996 and 2001. However, there were additional options available for conscientious objectors. Whilst not being given exemptions to National Service, there was a system put in place where any person who did not wish to bear arms owing to their personal belief system could still serve the country by means of a co-operative system. One of this system's alternatives was for the person in question to travel to the former French colonies Niger and Mali in West Africa, and serve by taking part in a teaching programme. It was this which Nicolas' father had opted to do. Nicolas' father held left-wing views, and as such this seemed to him a better alternative to joining the military.

After Nicolas' father had finished serving his time in his teaching post, he returned to France in order to attend university, where he had decided that he would begin studies in chemistry. It was during this time that the infamous 1968 Student Protests were taking place in several countries across the world. These protests were extreme and often turned violent in nature. They represented a worldwide escalation of social conflict, characterised by increasing rebellions against the military (against the Vietnam war in particular) and the government and bureaucracy. The events for these protests were further instigated by social factors, such as the fight against capitalism, sexism, imperialism, and even the death of the revolutionary leader Che Guevara.

At the time, Nicolas' father had substantial involvement with these radical left-wing groups, and even on occasion had encounters with the infamous terrorist Ilich Ramírez Sánchez, better known as 'Carlos the Jackal', who was imprisoned in 1997 and is currently serving several life sentences. In France, at the height of these protests, the university students, including Nicolas' father, had been closely linked with the 'Wildcat' strikes, which were rumoured to have up to 10 million workers involved; it was said that at one point they had the potential power and capability to overthrow the French Government. It was during this time where Nicolas' father, while still at university, had met the woman who would become his partner, and subsequently, Nicolas' mother.

Nicolas' grandparents on his mother's side of the family were from a small coastal town called Dahouet in Brittany on the north-western coast of France. His grandfather had earned his living by means of being a fisherman. His grandparents on his father's side were from Paris, and this particular grandfather had earned a living working for a bank corporation. It was this line of work in which Nicolas' father opted to undertake a career, once he had left university. His study of chemistry was seemingly abandoned in pursuit of a career in the financial sector, and as a result, Nicolas' father went to work for the same banking firm in which his grandfather was employed. The role that his father took involved IT networking within the bank, and as a result, the bank would send him to various countries around the world in order to roll out the banking networking systems for the company.

One such undertaking for the bank took Nicolas' future parents to the African country of Cameroon. Whilst his father was deployed in Cameroon, his mother, on the 22nd of March 1972, gave birth to Nicolas Claux. He was born in a rural hospital in the capital of Cameroon, on the outskirts of Yaoundé. The deployment of the family to Cameroon lasted for approximately one year after the birth of Nicolas. It was a time in where Nicolas' mother found life difficult. Despite his father being inundated with his work for the bank, his mother despised being a young mother in a foreign and under-developed African country. Life was tough for his mother, and as a result, she could not wait to leave Cameroon.

For the first few years of Nicolas' life, he and his family travelled from one country to another, all under the blanket of his father's role and obligation to his work for the bank, and often living in a particular country for up to two years at a time. After leaving Cameroon, the family went to Geneva in Switzerland, and the family lived there until Nicolas was approximately three years old. From Geneva, the family then were stationed in London, where yet again his father would undertake a project for the bank, rolling out the company network. It was at this time that the young Nicolas Claux uttered his first words. Perhaps owing to the influence of songs on the radio and programmes on the television, these words were actually in English, despite his French parentage. His father's assignment in London lasted until Nicolas was five years old, at which point the family finally returned to France.

Once the family were back in France, they settled in the 15th District of Paris, in the southwest region of the city known as the Rue de Lourmel. This is an upmarket section of Paris, hosting the Tour Montparnasse skyscraper and the Andre Citroen, which is situated along the banks of the River Seine and draws in a great number of families and tourists each year. As Nicolas was coming up to six years old at this time, it was here where he first began to attend school. It is from this time that Nicolas has his first recollections of making friends with other children. Due to the fact that up to that point he had moved location a great deal, he found it increasingly difficult to mix well socially with others. Due to his inability to get on with others, the number of friends he accumulated was comparatively small: his social circle at school comprised roughly three or four friends at the most.

Nicolas at around 8 or 9

Nicolas' memories of his interactions with friends are not as in-depth as other children's tend to be. In Nicolas' opinion, memories are attached to emotions, or even emotional times; as he was the only child of a family that did not believe in showing emotions, there were infrequent occasions when memories such as these could be attached to an emotive state.

Nicolas' mother, in particular, was raised in an environment where the showing of emotions was regarded in a negative light. In accordance with her upbringing, the vocalising of statements such as 'I love you' would have been seen as showing signs of weakness. It was these misguided ideals that she implemented in her emotional care of her son, Nicolas.

It wasn't as though Nicolas was 'abused' in the general understanding of the term; physically, he appears to have always been in general good health during his childhood, with no real or significant problems as such. The only signs that could be seen as being abusive by today's standards were that, during Nicolas' formative years as a child, he was given absolutely no emotional support whatsoever from his mother. This was coupled with his father's frequent absences due to work-related travel; his father was seldom around physically, to say nothing of the obvious void in terms of emotional support.

There have been studies undertaken in children between the ages of five and ten years old, who have in the past been emotionally neglected. These studies have highlighted evidence that this form of emotional neglect has had a negative effect on the cognitive, language and behavioural functionality of the children exposed to it, with both internalisation and externalisation of these behavioural issues or problems as they develop in years. This has led to childhood and then adult adversity later on in life. This is, in fact, a form of what could be deemed as maltreatment, due to potential neuro-developmental issues. Therefore, intervention at a young age, or in the neurologically formative years, is now regarded as a key factor as a preventative measure. Owing to the absence of his father for large portions of time, and the emotional distancing from his mother, this issue was in fact suspected in Nicolas' case, but unfortunately it was never fully diagnosed.

As a result of this emotional maltreatment of Nicolas, coupled with the fact that the family had moved around from one country to another at regular intervals, he was exposed to what would be a very lonely and disconnected childhood. He would have felt that he had no ability to emotionally respond to various circumstances, having had no opportunity to build his understanding or develop tools to maintain adequate social relationships. As a result, he would have not been able to understand how to recognise the appropriate emotional trigger which would invoke a measured emotional response.

As far as Nicolas was concerned at the time, however, the thought of being lonely did not hinder his mental state. Up until that time, he had actually not had any particular set of circumstances where he could make accurate comparisons to other situations. An example that Nicolas has given is that a child blind from birth cannot miss having the sense of sight, having never have had the ability to see in the first place. In terms of Nicolas' emotional blindness, so to speak, he had never experienced the situation in which he wasn't alone, and as a result, he felt it impossible to have missed the company of other children, having never had this company in the first place. For Nicolas, the attempt at trying to raise any emotional response to this would ultimately draw a blank in terms of recognition. He would liken this to the same feeling that he would get when trying to visualise the road in front of him while walking through thick and dense fog. He did of course begin some friendships when he started school once his family had returned to Paris, but his inability to make strong childhood connections with others not only limited the number of children with which he felt that he could interact, but, as his strained set of school interactions were limited to the confines of the school, outside of the school term, on scheduled vacation times, Nicolas would spend this time alone once again. As a result, these vacation times were once again lonely times for the young Nicolas, and as a result, he was unable to trigger an emotional response related to this loneliness.

Nicolas was never able to take comfort or solace in any form of religion. Religion was not practised within his family's household. As a rule, a person's religious beliefs are generally inherited from those of their parents, or from other human interactions and connections that they encounter during their lives. As Nicolas' parents were both atheists, there was no inherited system of beliefs from which Nicolas could draw. In fact, as far as Nicolas is concerned, the entire concept of religion can be more likened to a projection of emotions, or emotional states; an example of this would be that once you had inherited religious beliefs from your parents, these would serve to trigger learned emotional states connected to religious subjects. In this case, with Nicolas, where there is a clear emotional void, in part with no concrete religious belief system in place within the household, there is nothing in which to trigger an adequate emotional connection or response. With that in mind, the concept of not being able to make any emotive response to any religious practice makes the entire concept of a 'God' impossible to create as an ideal. The entire aspect of religion, therefore, combined with the fact that no religious practices nor any concept of God were being taught within the school curriculum, made Nicolas quite critical about any religious belief system.

The first glimpse of anything relating to religious or spiritual terminology that Nicolas was able to make any connection with, came at the age of approximately six years old, when his father had returned from one of his work-related trips abroad – in this instance from Thailand. Following this trip to Bangkok, Nicolas' father had brought back with him photographs of his visit to Wang

Saen Suk Monastery Garden, better known as 'Hell Park'. His father showed him all of the photographs that he had taken on the trip, but it was the photos of this park in particular which caught the eye of his son. The photographs showed pictures of tall statues of thieves and criminals, depicted in what was deemed 'Buddhist Hell': for example, there were photographs of sculptures of people who had been burned to ashes, had their eyes gouged out, or even having been thrown to the wolves to be eaten alive.

The photographs of the Buddhist Hell statues that his father took while in Thailand fascinated Nicolas a great deal, and as a result of being shown these particular photographs, two things happened for the first time. One was that, for the first time that Nicolas could recollect, he was able to make an emotional connection to, or even with, his father. Up until that time, there had been no connection between the two of them, owing to his father's absence due to work commitments. The interest that Nicolas was able to show towards the photographs of the park that his father had taken, provided the very first opportunity in where Nicolas and his father had actually gained the means to bond as a father and son.

Wang Saen Suk Monastery Garden (taken in 2013)

The second thing that occurred was that, once again for the very first time, Nicolas had found himself feeling an emotional response or even emotional trigger towards what could be deemed a concept of religion or spirituality. It was actually this very emotional trigger which would be the beginning of Nicolas' morbid fascinations. The fascination would come to include death, Hell, Satanism (in particular Buddhist Satanism); anything, indeed, which could be deemed as the macabre. This particular fascination grew over the years; as there was no internet to speak of at the time, research into these subjects came in the form of reference books and other material in libraries and bookshops.

This fascination led Nicolas to begin to uncover the philosophies behind things such as African Voodoo and witch doctors: an interest potentially ignited, and certainly spurred on by the fact that Nicolas himself had been born in Cameroon. As a result, these and other dark arts, with a basis stemming from all cultures across the world, became an avid interest to Nicolas.

The years passed, and as a result, so did Nicolas' interest in the darker aspects of life and religion. At the age of approximately six or seven years old, during a family trip to London, England, Nicolas became acquainted with the works of the renowned occult author Dennis Wheatley. It was the works of Wheatley, such as the novel *The Devil Rides Out* and his non-fiction book *The Devil and All His Works*, which captured the attention of a young Nicolas Claux. Nicolas was fascinated by these writings, and in turn, he became engaged in a quest to discover more books on the subject of the occult. It was from this desire for research that Nicolas first encountered the subject of Pazuzu. An ancient Mesopotamian deity, Pazuzu was the king of the demons of the wind and the bearer of storms and drought. Nicolas found himself being immediately drawn to this ancient religious figure: a statue he saw triggered a strong emotional and religious response from within Nicolas. This discovery occurred long before Nicolas encountered the version of Pazuzu portrayed in the blockbuster movie *The Exorcist* (as discussed in Chapter 3).

This strong, emotional connection was not a fleeting response from Nicolas. In fact, it would be an emotional connection that has stayed with him to this day. Incidentally, the most famous statue of Pazuzu, sculptor Cuogli's monumental rendering of the Demon King, is on display at the Louvre museum in Paris, where Nicolas often had the opportunity to visit the work of art and bask in its ambience for himself.

Statue of Pazuzu in the Louvre museum

Art would come to play a major factor in the life of Nicolas, as we will come to discover later in the book. Nicolas began to seek out the images and paintings of the darker elements of religion and nature. He discovered paintings that became highly inspiring to him, such as the 'Witches' Sabbath': this painting, created by the great Spanish artist Francesco Goya, was classified under what would be later known as the 'The Witchcraft Paintings', and even linked to the 'Black Paintings'. It depicts the demon Baphomet as a goat figure, surrounded by a series of witches, and one of whom can be seen to be presenting a newborn baby in her arms, to the rest of the group, or coven. Once again, the contents of this dark painting represented one of the few elements or images that were able to invoke an emotional response from within Nicolas.

Goya's 'Witches' Sabbath'

It was at the age of nine years old, Nicolas would later recall, that he received what would be the first visual stimulus to create an emotional response within his own mind. The family had taken a routine vacation to the Alps, the mountain range famous for its magnificent scenery, and ample skiing opportunities. The area mountains, and the resort in which they were based, were all, as might be expected, blanketed in snow.

While his parents left Nicolas to his own devices inside the rented vacation accommodation, he found himself occupying his time by watching television. One channel in particular that he found himself watching showed trailers of new and upcoming movies, designed to entice a viewer to go out and watch these new movies for themselves. At this time, most of the movies on offer were the standard types: various French comedies and the latest *Star Wars* films, for example. However, there was one movie trailer in particular which caught Nicolas' attention: the one for the latest in the series of the *Phantasm* films. Nicolas was captivated by the macabre soundtrack of the film trailer. The trailer itself had images of tall men working in a graveyard and a funeral home, complete with what Nicolas understood to be an evil midget or alien, that went on to drill a hole into the forehead of another individual. And, further, the entire trailer seemed to be based around the concept of a massive, metallic-coloured sphere. It was only an introduction to the film, yet nevertheless, Nicolas found himself being utterly memorised by this trailer.

The visions of the images of this trailer, coupled with the seem-ingly haunting and macabre soundtrack that accompanied it, began to haunt the dreams of Nicolas soon after. At first, he had dreams, or even nightmares in which he would be peering down the white, marble corridors of a funeral home, curious as to what lay behind the plaques on the walls, which Nicolas would later learn were, in fact, cremation displays. In his dreams, while peering down the marble corridor, he would be chased and taunted by the metallic sphere, following his every move. It was not long, however, before the role in which Nicolas had found himself within his dreams was reversed: his position had evolved from the one being hunted to the hunter. In this dream world, it was Nicolas who began to pursue others with the use of this *Phantasm*-inspired metallic sphere.

From this point in time, Nicolas found the trailer of this *Phantasm* movie, coupled with the subsequent role-reversal within his dreams, to be a major influence on his perceptions of life. At the age of ten, Nicolas would arrive at what would essentially become the pivotal point in self-awareness and recognition: he defines this as his childhood coming to an untimely end.

A recent photograph of Dahouet

Every summer, up until the age of ten, Nicolas would spend some time at his maternal grandparents' house in the small coastal town of Dahouet. Despite Nicolas' inability to grasp many situations or secure connecting relationships on an emotional level, he was actually quite fond of these grandparents. In particular, he was very fond of his mother's father. During the months of July and August of each year, Nicolas found himself feeling the unfamiliar emotion of happiness. These were the only times that he can recollect from his childhood where he can make this statement with any sense of certainty.

Over the years Nicolas came to know the area in and around Dahouet extremely well, and during each summer, he would often go for long hikes along the cliff regions of the town, or submerge himself in the natural beauty of the region. This was a time when he was able to have constant and consistent interaction with other children of a similar age, as his cousins on his mother's side would quite often come to visit the area during those summer months. As stated previously, Nicolas did not have any siblings, and therefore it was during these summer months in which he was able to reconnect with family members other than his parents. He and his cousins would play in the surrounding areas of the small town, such as the small harbour, where fishermen would dock in between fishing expeditions. It was actually from this small harbour that Nicolas' grandfather would take Nicolas on several fishing excursions during the months of July and August each year.

It was during one particular trip to Dahouet in the summer of 1982, when Nicolas was ten years old, that things would ultimately change forever.

This year Nicolas travelled to Dahouet just as he had done in so many years prior to this. The only difference this time was that he began to notice that his grandfather seemed considerably less energetic than he had done in previous years, to the point where he actually appeared exhausted most of the time. On one day in particular, Nicolas wanted to play a game of badminton with his grandfather. His grandfather, though reluctant to play owning to fatigue, obliged Nicolas in this instance, proceeded to pick up his badminton racket and started to play the game with Nicolas.

Whilst playing the game with Nicolas, his grandfather collapsed directly in front of him and appeared unresponsive. As a result, an ambulance was called to the property, and his grandfather was subsequently taken to hospital. His mother and grandmother, who were also at the property at the time, proceeded to follow in suit to the hospital, clearly concerned as to the well-being of Nicolas' grandfather, who by this point had been admitted to hospital. After a few days had passed, while the family was readying themselves for a visit to the hospital to check up on his recovery, they received a telephone call from the hospital informing them that Nicolas' grandfather had passed away during the night owing to complications resulting from the stroke he had suffered while playing with Nicolas.

Naturally, the family were in a state of shock and grief. Nicolas could see the emotional state that his family were in at the time, and in turn, he mimicked the state of emotions that the family were displaying. In truth, however, he could not understand or comprehend the actual emotions for himself. What Nicolas found himself actually experiencing emotionally on the inside was a sense of detachment rather than one of grief.

In the nights that followed the death of his grandfather, his mother and grandmother would sit in a room and talk for a long time. On one night in particular, Nicolas had crept from his room, late at night, and had proceeded to listen in on the conversation between the pair. It was as he eavesdropped on this conversation that Nicolas heard his own mother blaming him for the death of his grandfather. She accused him of killing his grandfather by making him play a game of badminton. As she was concerned, young Nicolas was solely responsible for his grandfather's sudden collapse and subsequent death.

Nicolas went back to his room, having clearly heard his mother's mindset. The mind of the ten-year-old Nicolas began to process the things that he had just heard. There was a mix of emotions running through his mind; however, the feeling of guilt about the death was not one of them. The only guilt that Nicolas was able to relate to was that he was not feeling the grief or sadness that the rest of his family seemed to display towards his grandfather's passing. What Nicolas found himself feeling, in fact, was a sense of pride within himself, should he be the person responsible for someone else dying. He felt empowered by the fact that he apparently possessed the ability to control life and death. He deemed this to be an important factor in the process of life, and as a result, this revelation gave Nicolas an overwhelming pride about who he was.

On the day of his grandfather's funeral, the mood was sombre, as would be expected considering the circumstances. The funeral itself was planned to be a small ceremony, held in the local funeral home. What came as the most dramatic surprise was that, travelling to the funeral home, Nicolas' mother actually refused to share a car with her son, still harbouring feelings of resentment towards Nicolas and laying the sole blame for the death at the feet of her own son. As a result, Nicolas was forced to travel to the ceremony at the funeral home in a different car. He was subsequently placed in a car among people that he did not know and was thus forced to travel to the ceremony to all intents and purposes on his own.

Inside the funeral home itself, his mother continued to maintain her sense of emotional distance from Nicolas, refusing to let him sit next to her during the ceremony. The resentment and anger she harboured towards Nicolas were clear for all in attendance to see. Nicolas was therefore forced to sit apart from his immediate family.

Nicolas approached the coffin in which his grandfather was being laid to rest, and whilst he was able to catch a glimpse of his departed grandfather in his coffin, he did not in actual fact pay much heed to the still body. What caught the attention of Nicolas inside the funeral home was not the grief of the occasion, nor even the religious aspects of the ceremony, but the funeral home itself. Nicolas did try to invoke emotions or feelings towards the ceremony, but in truth he was distracted by the physicality of the funeral home. The room was dimly lit, and there were old-fashioned drapes adding to the décor of the room, but what was really encapsulated for Nicolas in this instance was the energy that the room seemed to possess. The room seemed to have an energy that acted independently from that of the mourners currently dwelling inside of the building, and to Nicolas, this was a completely new and fascinating sensation.

It was a sensation that he could not accurately describe in words. It was as though he was hearing the voices of the dead, speaking to him through a series of vibrations, vibrations which seemed to act like an independent pulse. The voices could only be heard by him. The physical feeling that most closely describes this would be to imagine standing directly next to the main speakers at a music concert, feeling every single vibration of the sounds travel throughout the body, connecting to your inner core, and all the while being caught in the epicentre of a cyclone or tornado. This may get close to the physicality of these feelings, without counting what it meant to feel all of these sensations on a spiritual level. The outer distractions of the funeral ceremony did not seem to matter anymore; it was the atmosphere, the sensations, and the voices of the dead that had Nicolas' full attention at this point.

Nicolas knew then and there that it felt right or correct for him to be there. This was his rightful place in life. It was as if all the pieces of his childhood had come together to this one point in time where it could provide an explanation for the puzzle of his life. It was Nicolas' ground zero, if you like: his spiritual awakening. And it was within this spiritual awakening that Nicolas was able to discover his true *Dharma*. His *Dharma* lay among the dead.

TWO

ADOLESCENCE
The Journey to Self-Discovery

THE VERY DEFINITION of psychosis is an impaired relationship with reality. Psychosis displays the symptoms of various serious mental disorders, with a high percentage of these symptoms developing in the formative years of youth. Patients tend to develop a distorted vision of reality, even suffering sensory experiences such as hallucinations. One of the proven underlying causes for this type of psychosis is emotional detachment, which in turn can lead to a form of Post Traumatic Stress Disorder (PTSD) or even Borderline Personality Disorders (BPD).

Depending on the level of psychosis, patients of these disorders can develop abstract coping mechanisms, quite often leading to a detachment from reality, and even seeing or hearing things that others cannot. These views and perceptions of reality in patients are near-on impossible for others to share. They are delusions that can, at times, cause distress in the patient and as a result can cause a severe change in behaviour, in turn leading to negative traits such as self-harm and obsessive compulsions. Quite often, psychosis can masquerade as Obsessive Compulsion Disorder (OCD) in patients.

A patient of this nature will have the inability to emotionally regulate their feelings from a young age in life. A child experiencing social exclusion would be a prime candidate for this type of emotional or mental disorder. What a child during their formative years develops as their learned state of beliefs would then, in turn, develop as a form of migration of these beliefs into adult life. They would therefore come to rely on this view of the world, as it is all that they would have known or understood. As a result, it could develop into their entire focus, even influencing their levels of understanding.

Without intervention by either therapy or medication, the obsessive traits that they would have come to develop in their formative years would then be ever-present in later life. These traits would be their epicentre and sole understanding in terms of functionality and understanding, in the same manner in which a person who suffers from depression (without a form of intervention) is unable to shift their focus out from within their depressive state, regardless of the fact that others may view the patient's surroundings as being either positive or negative. It is that state of depression that becomes the entire focus for the patient, and quite often they feel consumed by this, unable to shift their attention from the depressed state on which they are solely focused. The depression therefore becomes the epicentre of their particular state of mind. Therefore, a person who displays obsessive traits under the banner of psychosis is likely to be unable to shift their focus and attention from what has become the centre of their understanding.

True crime perpetrators from the past such as Ted Bundy and Jeffrey Dahmer have quite often been labelled as psychopathic in nature, under examination from various psychologists and psychiatric studies. However, most of these studies have focused on the period after they had already been apprehended by law enforcement agencies. It is true that a retrospective view of their childhoods has been presented to the public; however, very little has ever been brought to the surface as to what the parents or even school teachers did in order to highlight potential signs or symptoms as they presented themselves. Given both men's individual psychological diagnoses, there would have almost certainly have been key indicators present within each of these individuals relating to a potential diagnosis, which could then have been identified.

Therefore, it could be speculated that, given the proper attention to any of these individuals during the time of their formative years, and complete attention as to their behaviours at a younger age, adequate intervention could even have prevented their specific crimes later in their lives.

The thoughts and feelings of an individual suffering from psychosis, by definition, will be what defines the main focus of their attention. Therefore, whatever each individual has identified for themselves as an emotional trigger has the potential to activate their psychotic behaviour.

Following the death of Nicolas' grandfather in the summer of 1982, the family were preparing to embark on yet another excursion outside of France, once again due to Nicolas' father's work for the banking firm. This time the location was to be Portugal. However, between the period following the death of his grandfather and the family's relocation to Portugal, with the relationship between Nicolas and his mother still seemingly strained (as she continued to blame Nicolas for his grandfather's death), Nicolas was sent to live with his uncle in a different region of Paris from the family home. He would remain under the care of his uncle until all of the plans for the relocation were confirmed, and the family was ready to depart.

At the time when Nicolas was living with his uncle, there was a lot of media coverage regarding the case of Issei Sagawa, a Japanese student who had been studying in Paris. The year before, in 1981, Sagawa had invited a classmate to dinner. This was Renée

Hartevelt, a Dutch national who was also studying in Paris at the time. Sagawa had made the invitation under the pretence of translating poetry. Instead, he had shot and killed her. Afterwards, he engaged in necrophilia with the young woman's corpse. He then proceeded to dismember her body and engaged in cannibalism by eating small pieces which he had removed from it.

Following Renée Hartevelt's death, a popular magazine by the name of *PHOTO* had unscrupulously obtained photographs of the mutilated corpse, having purchased them from an employee at the Paris morgue. The magazine then went on to publish twelve of these photographs in a limited edition, with the obscene photographs featured in a spread. The publication was, however, in violation of French law, which forbids the publication of photographs representing the body of a victim of murder. Subsequently, Jean Durieux, the editor and chief of *PHOTO* at the time of publication, was later jailed, despite not revealing who he had obtained them from.

The publication was therefore recalled from sale, with *PHOTO* ordered to retrieve all copies of the published edition (some 240,000 copies). However, this was not before Nicolas' uncle had obtained a copy. His uncle was more fascinated with owning a copy because the magazine was banned, rather than for the content that it was banned for.

Nicolas had heard about the magazine, and realised, during a conversation, that his uncle had obtained a copy. During a search of his uncle's magazine collection, he discovered the copy of the banned issue. He opened the magazine and gazed in wonder at the 12 black and white photographs that the issue published. It was the first time in his life that Nicolas had been exposed to pictures of this ilk.

The images conjured up strange feelings. As he gazed upon the photographs of the dismembered student, what he began to feel was not dissimilar to what he had felt when he gazed at the corpse of his grandfather in the funeral home in Brittany. There was, however, one distinction between the feelings that were conjured up inside Nicolas when he gazed at his grandfather's corpse, and those generated by the photographs of Renée Harteveld: the photos of the deceased student combined his feelings regarding his morbid fascination with death with a new sense of sexual arousal. This was the first time that Nicolas had felt any additional feelings with regard to this particular subject, as well as the first time a sexual element had been added to his ever-growing morbid curiosity.

To this day Nicolas states that he can close his eyes and in his mind still see the images with great clarity, and further still, he can remember how he felt inside while looking at the pictures for the first time. Little did Nicolas realise at the time, while gazing at the photographs, that this feeling was, in fact, the very first indication or sign of how his life would eventually unfold.

It was a strange and confusing time for Nicolas, as he understood that the feelings that he was having for these photographs and his morbid sense of curiosity were not normal compared to those of most other people. Especially so, when everybody else who looked at the photographs of the deceased student seemed to recoil in a sense of shock or horror at the mere sight of them. In addition, most people, as far as Nicolas was concerned, seemed to have a natural sense of disgust, and were highly judgemental in the direction of the perpetrator, Issei Sagawa. By contrast, Nicolas had no judgement about Sagawa and began to feel that he was the only person who was actually drawn towards the photographs themselves. As a result of this, Nicolas began to sneak the magazine to his bedroom at night in secret, so he was able to look at the photographs in private, and do so repeatedly. The truth is, despite the sense of recoil that others seemed to display towards the images, Nicolas actually enjoyed looking at them, and he would do so night after night, despite knowing that what he was doing would most certainly have been considered morbid, and quite different from what most people would consider normal.

A few months passed, and the day finally came when Nicolas and his parents were finally ready to depart for Portugal for his father's work expedition. The work that Nicolas' father was going to be doing in Portugal was the exact same work that he had been doing in places such as London or Geneva: the computer maintenance of the bank, and the rolling out of new or upgraded bank networking systems. The difference between this relocation and that of previous employment campaigns was that, instead of relocating for a couple of months at a time, this time the family would have to relocate from France for a period of four years.

While Nicolas' father was set to be working out of the bank's main branch, located in the centre of the capital city Lisbon, the family were to live in a bank-owned apartment in the seaside town of Cascais, approximately 30 minutes' drive from the centre of Lisbon. The apartment was located directly opposite the main train station of Cascais. It was in this apartment that Nicolas and his parents would reside for the next two years.

In the apartment in Cascais, the attic of the apartment had been converted to a bedroom. It was this attic conversion that Nicolas would have as his living quarters for the next two years. The bedroom was, in a manner of speaking, quite separated from the rest of the household. This separation from the household, combined with the fact that his mother was still unable to overlook the blame she felt towards Nicolas after his grandfather had died and so continued her emotional distancing towards him, meant that Nicolas' parents rarely decided to check in on him, or even find out what he seemed to be occupying his time with.

In Portugal, Nicolas attended a school that was designed primarily for the academic needs of French expats in the area. However, due to the high standard of education at the school, the attendees of the school ended up being comprised of children from the families of wealthy Portuguese locals, such as doctors and high-profile personalities who wished to obtain a higher standard of education for their children.

As a result of this, surprisingly, Nicolas found himself being the only actual French-speaking person in his class. This, once again, made it extremely difficult for him to fit in with his classmates. In addition, the children, and even the majority of the people in the area, seemed to set their mood according to Portugal's bright and sunny weather, and were actually very friendly as a rule. This was a trait or concept that Nicolas found himself to be very uncomfortable with. Further to this, the children of the school, and indeed the remainder of the local population as well, seemed to be obsessed with football. As Nicolas detested all forms of team sports, this served to create yet further divisions between himself and his classmates.

Nicolas tried to adapt to his new surroundings and school, but he began to feel that his efforts in doing so seemed to be hopeless. The differences between Nicolas and his classmates gave rise to the feeling within Nicolas of a rejection from those around him. Nicolas had the impression that, once again, he was the outsider within his school. This was further enhanced by the fact that in addition to being the only native French speaker in his class, he was also unable to speak or understand Portuguese. Nicolas felt that he would be teased or made fun of by the other children in the school, and as a result of this, he began to feel extremely isolated once again.

In order to fill his time, and distance himself from any feelings of isolation, Nicolas began to read a great deal. At first he would obtain his reading material by visiting the local library in Cascais. Nicolas found this library to be of great use, considering that, for the size of the town, the library was quite extensive and had a large selection of reading material from which Nicolas could choose. The genres of fictional horror stories and of true crime seemed to fascinate Nicolas the most. He would spend hours upon hours reading and studying his chosen subjects. One particular true crime story that held a great deal of interest for Nicolas was that of Jack the Ripper. Recalling himself as a child of 13 years old, Nicolas believes that this particular subject represented his first real and consistent interest in the true crime genre. His interests were more than just curiosity on the subject. His interest in Jack the Ripper began to evolve into more than just studying the stories behind the infamous murders in the East End of London. It was the methodology of the murders which held a fascination for Nicolas. What is more, since the Ripper murders remained unsolved, the idea of being able to commit the crimes or murders without being detected or apprehended by the police became a particular point of interest to Nicolas.

It was during this time that Nicolas discovered a magazine named *Fangoria*. This magazine, launched in 1979, allowed horror fans to obtain the latest news and information pertaining to the release of new horror films. The magazine gave reviews of newly released films, as well as having in-depth coverage of the actors and characters from these horror films. Nicolas was able to obtain copies of this informative magazine, and since Nicolas had been given a television and VCR for his bedroom, he could use the magazine to get insights as to which horror films he might have a particular interest in viewing.

Other than visiting the library, Nicolas had very little to do in his time spent outside of his school. Therefore, during the entirety of his spare time that he spent outside of the local library, he began to rent and watch some of the horror movies which he had discovered in *Fangoria*, as well as continue to read and study the stories from the books which he had borrowed from the library. He took in as much detail as he could from both these sources of interest.

Nicolas' studies at school had begun to deteriorate, along with his grades. The social isolation that he felt while he was at school, combined with his fascination for true crime studies and the series of horror films that he had been watching, meant that the world of horror had not only started to take over his life, but had now become a point of continuous research and study, rather than a mere time-fulfilling interest. During his time at school he had begun to create fantasies rather than pay attention to his school studies. The fantasies were all related to his out-of-school interests, and it was not long before Nicolas' fantasies had begun to evolve into killing his classmates.

He fantasised about following one, or even several, of his classmates into the bathroom at school and slashing their throats. He held onto this fantasy to the point where he actually had the entire sequence of potential events completely planned out, to the very last detail, so that he could bring his fantasies to life, should he wish to.

Nicolas became so preoccupied with these fantasies, to the point that his thoughts of re-enacting the potential events took over his entire thought process while he was at school. This intense distraction was the main reason why his attention had begun to steer away from his school work, resulting in his standard of grades deteriorating. Nicolas, however, did not care about his grades at that time; his fantasies had taken over as an obsession within him, so much so that he had even begun to bring a knife to school, should he ever feel that he wished to bring his inner desires to life.

Nicolas had become so obsessed with the thought of killing his classmates that he was unable to think about anything else. It was these obsessional thoughts that a psychiatrist would later come to identify as what was, in fact, the very beginning of Nicolas' psychosis disorder, and as such, would be the initial stages of what would be his 'psychosis process'. Such a mindset means that the person suffering from this particular disorder is unable to extricate themselves from their thought processes, regardless of how much they actually attempt to. It is in this exact psychosis process that convicted killers, such as Jeffrey Dahmer, for example, found himself becoming the victim of his thoughts, where the desire to carry out his fantasies became so severe that he was mentally unable to resist the urge to act out his fantasies in reality.

Nicolas found himself unable to escape his own particular thought process. In addition, the severity of his fantasies seemed to be increasing, by way of sinister thoughts that he was having. The series of returning thoughts on the subject would continually crash, like repetitive waves, against his mental landscape, to the point that his obsession would dominate his thought process and potentially paralyse any form of a healthy social life. It was this understanding of his own mental state of mind which made it easier for Nicolas to identify with convicted murderers, such as Jeffrey Dahmer, and the perhaps even more notorious Ted Bundy: Nicolas felt he was able to identify with the thought patterns of these individuals, by way of studying their respective actions. This is a mindset which, not unlike depression, would be difficult for most people to understand, if they have not experienced those specific feelings for themselves.

The school that Nicolas was attending had noticed that there was a change in his behavioural patterns, as well as the clear indication of his deteriorating grades. Aas a result, Nicolas' parents were called to the school for a meeting with the school's headmaster. The meeting, despite being held with good intentions, came to nothing. The main reason for this was that Nicolas' mother, still emotionally distant from Nicolas, was also experiencing similar adjustment problems to Nicolas: she was also unable to speak Portuguese, and found herself experiencing feelings of isolation in the coastal town. As a result of this, she had begun to show signs of depression. The combination of this depression, along with the inability to emotionally connect to Nicolas, meant that she was unable to fix her focus on the well-being of her son at that time. Further to this, Nicolas' father was extremely busy and preoccupied with his work for the banking firm, and therefore was not physically available as much as he would have liked to be to give full attention to the apparent issue at hand.

There was also the fact that there would be great difficulty in finding a therapist that would be able to converse in French, and as a result, the family had basically begun to hope that the problem would get better on its own.

Without the aid of a mental health professional, Nicolas was unable to divert his thoughts from his fantasies, and consequently remained committed to his morbid obsessions. The consummation of his obsessions, plus the fact that he had actually grown to enjoy his isolation, allowed Nicolas to remain within what he terms as his own self-built bubble, and remain able to focus on his interests. The isolation meant that Nicolas did not actually have any friends; in his mind, no friends meant less potential drama, and therefore less distraction from how Nicolas preferred to occupy his spare time.

As the years moved on, Nicolas got to the age when it would be normal practice for a teenager to start making use of their social skills. Having noticed people of his age group doing this, he attempted to follow suit. In truth, however, Nicolas was not really concerned whether he was successful at this or not. What other people were doing was of little consequence to him. Having failed somewhat in this respect, Nicolas felt that he identified more with that of a French philosopher that he had been studying, Albert Camus. To be more precise, Nicolas felt a deeper connection to a character from one of Camus' works, who was thought to have murdered his own mother, as a result of which the character had felt alienated from the rest of the human race. This was exactly how Nicolas perceived his own role within society.

Nevertheless, Nicolas did make an attempt to set aside his obsessions and interests in morbid tales of death and true crime and attempted to create a social circle for himself by getting involved in role-playing games with other teenagers of the same age: games such as 'The Call of Cthulhu' and the ever-popular 'Dungeons and Dragons'. Nicolas was able to temporarily set aside his obsessions and partake in these games; however, as is the nature of obsession, this could not last for any great length of time, and his interest in these games would soon become overshadowed once more by his personal fantasies.

A short while later, the family moved from the coastal town of Cascais, and into another bank-owned apartment. This, however, was in the centre of Lisbon, in what was considered to be an upmarket section of the city, very close to the famous bull-fighting arena, the Campo Pequeno Bullring. Following the departure of the family from Cascais, Nicolas' interest in role-playing games had departed as well. He once again recalled to the forefront of his mind his previous interests in morbid subjects: interests such as horror movies and books relating to death, and images or art in a similar vein. Now his interest in horror films had broadened to include films from different countries such as Russia, where the events of the films were depicted in a far darker and gruesome manner.

At this time, Nicolas discovered a large encyclopaedia that was devoted entirely to films made up to 1983. The films were listed and described in chronological order, and contained reviews, descriptions, and plot lines from famous horror production companies such as Britain's Hammer Studios. Each article was illustrated with a series of beautiful photographs or artwork from each film. One film which stood out to Nicolas in particular was a film made by the director of the original *Texas Chainsaw Massacre* director, Tobe Hooper: this was *Eaten Alive*. The cover art for this film was the killer chasing a young girl through the woods, wielding what appeared to be a scythe. After Nicolas had seen this cover art, he then began to fantasise about himself chasing his school classmates with a scythe, rather than the knife that had been the

weapon of choice in his previous fantasies. He thought about striking down and killing as many as possible of the school attendees
with the scythe: not dissimilar to the events which would later
come to fruition in the American high school at Columbine. Nicolas
would fantasise about killing his classmates in large numbers in
this manner, although without the firearms that the two teenagers
would utilise in Columbine several years later.

In 1988, after the family had moved into the centre of Lisbon,
and while the family were asleep at night, a burglar broke into the
family's apartment, through Nicolas' bedroom window. The burglar,
who had thought that the apartment was empty at the time, woke
Nicolas as he entered the room. Nicolas was naturally surprised
to see the burglar enter his room. He was not, however, scared or
frightened at the sight of the burglar. Instead, he simply asked the
burglar what he was doing there. The burglar, who hadn't expected
to encounter anyone in the room, was clearly startled, and as a
result, quickly exited the bedroom, but in doing so, accidentally
cut himself, leaving a large amount of blood, which had spilled
onto the surface of the apartment balcony. This experience did
not actually faze Nicolas in the slightest, and he calmly informed
his parents about what had just happened. The police were called;
surprisingly, they arrived at the apartment in great numbers, bran-
dishing machine guns. Nicolas could not understand why such a
big deal was being made out of the incident.

News of the intended burglary travelled fast, and owing to the
suspected 'trauma' that Nicolas had to endure from his ordeal,
his school were informed and were advised to tread cautiously in
their approach towards Nicolas, so as not to give him a tough time
in relation to his studies and general school life, or even to question him too much about the events of the burglary. News of the
burglary quickly spread throughout the school and the story had
soon evolved into exaggerated rumours that Nicolas had, in fact,
intentionally chased the burglar away. The teasing from other chil-

dren regarding Nicolas being 'weird' abruptly came to an end, and Nicolas was beginning to enjoy his newfound notoriety. Whereas in the past, Nicolas had brought a knife to school, thinking he might eventually act out his fantasies, he now brought an even bigger knife to school, not so much to satisfy his fantasies, but more as a means to brag and show off as the 'dispatcher of burglars'. He made sure that all of the children of the school were aware that he had the knife on him, which invoked a sense of fear of his presence. Nicolas admittedly thought this was indeed 'cool'.

While in the classroom, the big knife had fallen out of Nicolas' bag, and onto the floor. The staff member teaching at the time had noticed this, and as a result, Nicolas was once again sent to the headmaster's office. Once again, Nicolas' parents were called to the school for a meeting. As with the previous meetings between his parents and the school, it was again suggested that Nicolas be taken to see a therapist or psychiatrist of sorts. However, they still faced the same issues that they had done previously in not being able to obtain a French-speaking therapist. As a result, they again opted to do nothing regarding the situation. It was almost as though Nicolas' parents did not seem to care about the mental welfare of their son. In addition, the work which his father was undertaking at the bank was drawing to a close; as the family would be returning to France at the end of the school year and were already making preparations for relocating once again, immediate psychiatric care was not deemed to be necessary or even relevant.

As a result of being caught with the possession of the knife at school, Nicolas was suspended from school for a period of one week. Because this was a punishment that Nicolas did not actually mind, he paid very little attention to the fact that he was being punished for having possession of the knife. What Nicolas did pay attention to, on the other hand, were the looks that he seemed to be getting from fellow students and teachers. These reactions, he noted, almost gave the impression that Nicolas had instilled a sense of fear into them. As far as Nicolas was concerned, this type of reaction was a positive one to him, as it gave rise to a sense of empowerment over others. Therefore, in his mind, the punishment of being suspended was far less important to him than the sense of fear that his actions had instilled, so that the punishment seemed to have been completely worth it. In addition, somewhat surprisingly, the feelings of empowerment actually appeared to have satisfied his morbid fantasies, if only for a short period of time.

These morbid fantasies, although temporarily diminished, did not leave Nicolas in their entirety. He still had an internal conflict within his own persona; however, the decrease in obsession regarding his fantasies and obsessions did at least pave the way for Nicolas to focus on something other than his interests, for example his grades at school. In the entire time prior to being suspended, Nicolas' grades had always reflected the impression of a student who, while obtaining a satisfactory grade, could have done better. So there were clear indicators as to the fact that Nicolas could obtain high grades should he be inclined to give the schoolwork his full attention. So whereas his grades had perhaps suffered in the past because of his obsessions, he was, for this short while, able to satisfy his own mind, and keep him occupied with school work, at least until the family had returned to France.

THREE

THE RETURN TO FRANCE

Creating a Personal Identity

ANIMAL CRUELTY – The torturing of pets and small animals, especially during childhood, is known as zoo-sadism, and it is considered to be one of the signs of certain psycho-pathologies, including Antisocial Personality Disorder, and Psychopathic Personality Disorder.

It is said that a lot of murderers begin their path to murdering human beings by way of killing and torturing animals as children; certainly, animal cruelty as a child is an often-seen trait in those that later become serial killers.

Common examples of such murderers would be the often-cited Jeffrey Dahmer, also known as the 'Milwaukee Cannibal'. As an adult he murdered at least 17 people, but it was revealed that as a child Dahmer had in fact killed and dismembered cats and dogs and subsequently impaled their severed heads on spikes.

Another example would be Ian Brady, perhaps better known as the 'Moors Murderer', who killed at least five children in the 1960s. Brady admitted to killing his first cat when he was just 10 years old. He would also stone dogs to death and decapitate rabbits, before proceeding to develop to the murder of children.

Even the children Robert Thompson and Jon Venables were

discovered to have tied rabbits to the railway lines, just so that they could witness the rabbits being run over by trains, before their subsequent development to the vicious and gruesome murder of the toddler James Bulger in Liverpool in the early 1990s.

There is strong evidence, therefore, of links between cruelty to animals at a young age and going on to murder at a later age. Such key indicators, once they are known, should not be ignored.

During his time in Portugal, beginning in the coastal town of Cascais, Nicolas would have a fascination with the inner workings of small animals: he was not only fascinated by this during his time in Cascais, but he continued to be so when he moved to the centre of Lisbon, and then when he returned to Paris some years later.

In Cascais, Nicolas would satisfy his curiosity by capturing and subsequently dissecting small animals such as mice. There is evidence to suggest that Nicolas would torture a mouse with a hammer, scissors or even fire, then kill and dissect the small animal. When he moved from Cascais to the centre of Lisbon, he would develop this interest to include larger animals such as cats. While in Lisbon, Nicolas would frequent the large graveyards of the area, as these places seemed to provide Nicolas with a sense of peace, or even isolation, which he had come to enjoy over time. It was in places such as these that Nicolas would find such small animals and proceed to kill and dissect them.

Further to this, the graveyards fascinated Nicolas a great deal. He found the architecture of the buildings in the graveyard fascinating: not dissimilar to the types of buildings and the style of graves that he would have seen in the countless horror movies he had watched over the years, or even the images that he had witnessed in the horror movie books and magazines that he had read, in which the vampire graves and buildings surrounding them appeared almost identical to the ones that he was able to see within the various Lisbon graveyards. Nicolas found these graveyards to be peaceful places; further to this, the graves themselves, as well as the death symbols which were carved into the graves and gravestones, held particular interest for him. As he would spend a great deal of time by himself in isolation in Portugal, he would very often frequent these places.

In July 1988, at the end of the school year, Nicolas and his family returned to France, settling in Paris. Before the family had relocated to Portugal, he lived with his uncle in Paris, but this time he remained in the care of his parents. Upon the family's return to France, they stayed in a hotel in the 15th District of Paris, not far from the Eiffel Tower, in the Front de Seine region. The hotel was situated in a skyscraper, and the family had an apartment on the 25th floor of the building, giving them a magnificent view of the river and the Eiffel Tower itself.

During the months of July and August, Nicolas' mother made the annual commute to Brittany on vacation, to visit Nicolas' grandmother, as was customary when the family were living back in France. The distinction now was that his mother would make the journey to Brittany alone; after the death of his grandfather, Nicolas never returned to the region to visit the family, and therefore he remained with his father in Paris while his mother was on vacation.

One afternoon, while in the apartment in Paris, Nicolas was watching the news on television. The news report was telling the story of a funeral home in Florida, where investigators had discovered that several deceased bodies had been placed in the same coffin for burial or cremation; at the same time, those working in the funeral home had harvested some of the organs from the bodies prior to placing them into the ceremonial coffins. In fact, the flashes or depictions of the funeral home on the television reminded Nicolas of the funeral home in Brittany where his grandfather's funeral was held. The flashes of the plaques on the walls, and the coffins themselves, gave Nicolas the idea that, one day, he himself would like to work in a funeral home, as he found the whole idea of it fascinating. It was just a fleeting thought at the time, but an idea for the future, nonetheless.

In addition to the large number of bodies that were stacked inside single coffins, there were rumours circulating that the harvested organs, as well as sections of human flesh, had been removed from the bodies in Florida and had in fact been sold on to restaurants in the area for human consumption, evidently without the diners' knowledge. These were nothing more than rumours that had been spread, but it did seem to remind Nicolas of the Japanese student, Issei Sagawa, and the articles in *PHOTO* magazine which related the story of Sagawa's murder and cannibalisation of his victim. Nicolas, in turn, fell in love with the idea that the human flesh may actually have been sold on for human consumption: so much so, in fact, that when he visited the family's local butcher while shopping, he would gaze upon the diagrams on the walls depicting the various cuts of meat on a pig or cow and imagine that instead of the cow or pig, it would instead be a diagram of a human, showing which sections of the human body were the most suitable for various cuts of meat.

In September of 1988, the family moved to a new apartment in the 15th District of Paris. This apartment was once again funded by the bank where Nicolas' father worked. The apartment was two storeys high, and Nicolas once again found himself occupying a bedroom on the upper levels of the apartment, at the very top of the building. Nicolas' bedroom had its own entrance to the building and as a result he would be able to sneak out of the building at midnight, in a discreet manner, and return in the early hours of the morning, before anyone would have noticed that he had been missing for the night. This important detail will play a major role in Nicolas' story at a later time.

The flat was situated in a wealthy area in Paris; however, the majority of the inhabitants of the street or area were not of French descent. The street where they lived was extremely upmarket, filled with a vast amount of shops, owned mostly by Lebanese and Iranian immigrants, with a clientele from largely wealthy backgrounds.

With the family having returned from Portugal at the end of the school year, the end of the summer of 1988 meant that Nicolas would have to return to school in September. Naturally, moving to a new area came with the necessity of having to attend a new school. This just happened to be the most famous high school in Paris, Lycée Molière: a school attended by the children of wealthy parents such as doctors, lawyers, and famous singers and actors. By attending a high school in France, Nicolas thought that for once he might not be subjected to the type of isolation that he had previously felt while attending school in Portugal, as this was now a school where he could speak his native French, and therefore seem like less of an outsider. However, from his very first day at his new school, he understood that this was not going to be the case: he once again felt as though he would not fit in with his new classmates. The majority of the students knew each other from having previously attended schools together, such as primary school. As Nicolas had spent the previous four years attending school outside France, he had not met any of the other students before, and as a result he had difficulty adapting to this new school and fitting in with his new classmates. Once again, his feelings of isolation came to the forefront.

After having been left to his own devices for the majority of his time spent outside regular school hours, Nicolas once again began to feel a sense of morbid fascination creep to the forefront of his mind. One night, in particular, approximately two or three days into his new school term, his parents had decided to go away for the night, leaving Nicolas to his own devices for the evening. He decided to take a bath, and while doing so he began to self-harm by cutting into his own arm. He cut deep into the arm, as deep as he possibly could, in order to see his own flesh. The wound did not hurt as Nicolas expected it to, as he was preoccupied with how far he could cut into his own flesh without causing too much damage. The wound was not designed to cause severe injury, but was rather meant as an experiment on his own body and flesh, and was therefore relatively superficial. Nicolas was extremely fascinated by the sight of his own blood falling into the water of the bath, finding that he actually liked the image that his blood made when mixed in with the bath water. While still in the bath, Nicolas decided to drink his own blood, and to his surprise he found that he liked the taste of it. However, there was more to his interest than just the taste of his blood. He found that his blood made him feel extremely alive, almost as though it was feeding him a kind of energy that was different from that of any other source than he had experienced prior to this moment.

Nicolas continued to self-harm as time went on, as he became fascinated with the blood which flowed from his wounds when he did. At school, Nicolas did make attempts to cover the wounds and resulting scars by wearing long-sleeved tops and occasionally covering the open wounds with bandages. However, despite covering the wounds, he would continue to pick at the resulting scabs, as well as at the clots of blood that arose from doing so; at times he would lick the blood or scabs that appeared at the opening of the wounds. As previously mentioned, Nicolas not only liked the taste of the blood but additionally liked the sensation of the energy that tasting his own blood provided him with. The trouble was that constantly opening and reopening the wounds meant that they took a longer time than usual to heal, which left much more severe scars as a result.

The students in his class did seem to notice the cuts and wounds, which gave them the general impression that Nicolas was crazy. This, however, was not an image which he seemed to mind, as it provided him with a sort of defence mechanism, as the students would leave him to his own devices. It was though, a defence mechanism with a sinister twist.

Nicolas would usually sit at the back of the class, almost as though he was a sinister outcast, keeping away from the other students, as they kept away from him: an arrangement which seemed to suit Nicolas. One particular day he was sat at the back, and rather than paying attention as to the lesson being given by the teacher at that point in time, he decided to lift his long-sleeved top, and begin to loosen the scabs on one of his fresher wounds on his arm. Not thinking that anyone was watching him, he began to lick the blood that emanated from the freshly opened wound. What he didn't realise was that a girl in the class, from the opposite side of the room, had been watching him do so, and when he looked up at the young girl, she seemed to have a look of horror on her face. Nicolas, not entirely sure of how to respond to her look of horror, decided to smile at her. What he didn't realise, until he saw a further look of disgust and horror in her reaction, was that on his teeth were the remnants of the blood and clots from his arm, and when he smiled at her, these remnants were predominantly on display to the terrified girl from across the room.

It was not long before the entire school had become aware of what Nicolas had been doing, in terms of taking in his own blood. As a result, it was not long before Nicolas got the reputation of having a sinister nature, as opposed to that of his fellow students. It was not long before Nicolas became known as 'That Kid'. However, this did not faze him in the slightest; as a matter of fact, he actually seemed to enjoy being looked at in this particular way. Nicolas was obsessed with blood: the patterns that blood made when it reacted with another surface, the consumption of his blood, and, in addition, the reactions that doing so seemed to attract. It was not long before Nicolas did not care in the slightest what other students said or even thought about it; he was not only content with what he was doing, he actually enjoyed it.

The news of these events spread like wildfire throughout the school: in terms of Nicolas' reputation, the rest of the students at the school now understood that Nicolas was indeed quite different from what they deemed to be normal. The social interaction between Nicolas and the rest of the students decreased further, and, as a result, his social isolation seemed to widen. However, this was not something that seemed to cause Nicolas much suffering. The world in which the high-class and wealthy children lived, especially in terms of their social activity and interaction, seemed to be vastly different from how Nicolas lived on a daily basis. He began to understand, from very early on in his high school career, that he would never be like the other children. Being alone, though, was something that Nicolas was used to, and as result, he was able to conduct his life, complete with his fascinations, without any hindrance.

What was important to Nicolas was that he had his bedroom, where he could partake in his favourite pastimes of studying occult books and watching horror films. He still had his television and VCR from his time in Portugal, and as such, he was able to rent many horror films, such as the ones that he had seen mentioned in the large encyclopaedia of horror films he had read while still in Portugal. He watched a lot of zombie films, amongst others. And owing to the fact that his parents once again left him alone and very seldom checked in on his activity, he began to watch a lot of pornographic films. In truth, he watched an extensive amount of films in both genres, and it was not long before the two types of film had become linked in his mind.

Indeed, the mixture of pornographic material and horror films became so interlinked, and the feelings that he felt within his own psyche soon became so in tune with one another, that there seemed to be the same set of emotional connections when he watched either of these genres. This was especially the case when there happened to be an aggressive or gruesome set of sexual scenes within the horror genre. These generated a fascination with his morbid obsessions, which were now mixed in with strong feelings of sexual arousal.

At the age of 16, Nicolas had seen the movie *Rampage* for the first time. The movie was directed by William Friedkin, the same person who directed the first and most famous *Exorcist* film. *Rampage*, based on the story of Richard Chase, the infamous cannibal dubbed 'The Vampire of Sacramento', is usually described as a courtroom thriller. In the film, the lawyers on both sides are trying to determine the perpetrator's ability to stand trial, conducting a back-and-forth debate about the sanity of the defendant. However, in the film, there is a scene where the actor portraying Chase is drinking blood at an altar which has a person nailed to it. The visual aspects of the scene left a large impression on Nicolas and, as a result, he began to gather an interest in the real-life Richard Chase himself.

It was *Rampage* that initially led Nicolas to view other films directed by William Friedkin, in particular the infamous blockbuster movie, *The Exorcist*. Nicolas had previously been exposed to the demonic imagery of Pazuzu – the entity which takes over a child's body in *The Exorcist* – but the film itself, focused as it was on Satanic possession, also struck a chord of interest within Nicolas. As a result, it inspired him to begin researching more into the subject matter itself, as well as paying a visit to the Louvre Museum, where he was able to see the iconic statue of Pazuzu in person for the very first time.

The interest generated by the films caused Nicolas to widen his search for books relating to the occult and Satanism. At the time, there were three prominent book stores in the Notre Dame area specialising in books of this nature. Therefore, leading on from when he first found his father's copy of the Dennis Wheatley book *The Devil Rides Out* (described in Chapter 1), he began to increase his knowledge of such books and build upon his interest in Satanism. With each book that he read, he felt an even stronger connection to Satanism, and due to the time that he had spent in isolation, he was able to further piece together the pieces of his own puzzle and build a solid foundation for his interests and beliefs.

In his quest for Satanic knowledge and through the countless *grimoires* (magic textbooks) that he read, Nicolas discovered the work of the French Luciferian warlock, Octave Sieber. Sieber was, in fact, known as a professional warlock and would be hired for television shows covering his specialist subject, Black Magic. When Sieber gave tours of the famous Paris catacombs, he apparently stole skulls from there. There were also rumours that Sieber had been hired as a professional warlock by the infamous French serial killer Pierre Chanal, who, in exchange for Sieber's services, would give Sieber videos of his victims being murdered on film. These rumours fascinated Nicolas a great deal; however, at this stage there is no way to verify if they were true, owing to the fact that Sieber has since passed away, while Pierre Chanal committed suicide by hanging himself in his prison cell.

Whereas many modern Satanists find their route to Satanic worship via the common route of listening to Devil-inspired heavy metal, or even the more directly Satanic 'black' or 'death metal' music, this was not the case for Nicolas. He found his way in through intense studies of occult books, and even from a series of studies relating to African books regarding voodoo and black magic. (This may owe something to the fact that he was born in Cameroon.)

A natural progression for those interested in Satanism would be through what is considered to be dark and sinister imagery, namely images usually depicted in places such as cemeteries and the buildings within the burial grounds. As Nicolas had already gained an interest in places such as these, owing to the images he held onto from the time of his Grandfather's death, and the visit to the funeral home, this was a simple connection for him to move towards. This was helped by the fact that Nicolas had easy access to the outside world at night via his own entrance to the apartment building, and so Nicolas started to visit these places in Paris for himself.

There are quite a few such places in Paris which Nicolas could frequent: 14 in total, to be precise. The most famous are Père Lachaise cemetery in Montmartre and the cemeteries of Montparnasse. It was the latter that Nicolas would frequent most. He would quite often attend the cemeteries at dusk, having felt as if he was drawn towards the burial grounds in a way that could only be described as if by some form of spiritual magnet. The grounds themselves held huge monoliths and awe-inspiring sculptures that even those not drawn towards the imagery of death would find astonishing. At the Père Lachaise grounds, there was a set of stairs at the entrance to the crematorium dome in the centre of the cemetery, which led down under the ground of the building. Nicolas received the shock of his life – not in terms of being startled, but more so in the fact that the stairs resembled, in his mind, an almost identical vision of the stairs that he had remembered from the trailer of the movie *Phantasm* while he was on vacation as a child. Nicolas spent hours upon hours in the grounds, often up to three times a week, just soaking up the atmosphere and energy which the burial grounds provided him with. It was as though it were another significant spiritual awakening for him; he was drawn to places such as these. He felt that the pieces of the puzzle were coming together once again and knew that there, within the cemetery grounds, was the place he was meant to be.

FOUR

A RETURN TO PARIS

Initial Experiences and Discoveries

THE EMOTION OF Envy. The process of how this feeling impacts the mindset of a person who is impaired by any form of psycho-pathological disorder would be very different from that of a person who is without such impaired disorders. It has already been noted that convicted murderers became 'victims of their own thoughts', as it is termed, owing to their compulsions. To take the example of Jeffrey Dahmer, he did not have the mental ability to stop himself from engaging in a process where he would act out his fantasies in real life.

This is where envy plays its significant role in the devolution of a murderer. Dahmer, over and above his desire to engage in acts of cannibalism and murder, craved the companionship of his victims. His envy of what he perceived to be his victims' solid foundation of companionship with an intimate partner as a constant in their lives, gave rise to his efforts where he would drug his victims as a means to incapacitate them, and then proceed to drill into their skulls so that he could render his victims in a zombie-like state, so that they would ultimately not leave him, thus diminishing the envy he felt towards others. We now of course know that Dahmer's victims would ultimately die from their wounds, therefore creating the necessity for his murderous cycle to continue.

Police mugshot of Jeffrey Dahmer, 1991

Dylan Klebold, who was one of the young gunmen involved in the infamous Columbine High School shootings in Colorado in April 1999, was also driven by a sense of envy. After the massacre had ended and Klebold had taken his own life by means of a self-inflicted gunshot wound immediately thereafter, his journal was discovered. It was in this journal that Klebold wrote about witnessing the 'jocks' of his school, who would be enjoying the social successes that he was unable to obtain for himself. In addition, Klebold further noted as to how much fun these 'jocks' would be having as a result of their social successes, which was in stark contrast to that of his own life and social standing – so much so that Klebold had noted that he did not feel as though he was able to properly function as a human being. Klebold's envy of the 'jocks' seemingly laid the foundations for his anger and his antipathy, which would in turn spur him to his brutal and murderous rampage within the school grounds.

Even the person who was widely considered to be the most notorious serial killer of modern times, Ted Bundy, had deep-rooted manifestations of envy. While his earliest crimes are quite often overshadowed and subsequently overlooked owing to the nature and brutality of his abductions and murders, it has to be noted that Bundy began his criminal journey as a 'peeping Tom'. When he was in his teens Bundy would often spy on co-eds and other young girls through windows. Bundy's voyeurism stemmed from an envy of the girls that he was unable to obtain through the natural progression of courtship. In addition, Bundy's crimes of shoplifting from stores at an early age were derived from an envy of desiring items that he was unable to afford for himself. Therefore, in both of these instances, it is envy that is seemingly the main catalyst for what became the beginning of his criminal exploits. Which, as we all know, would later manifest further into his infamous series of murders.

Envy is quite often overlooked as a major catalyst in the progression of crime, once the crimes themselves, especially in murder cases, become the centre stage for attention in the media. However, in the psyche of a criminal mind, the trait or emotion of envy is not one that should be overlooked. Envy can manifest itself in a variety of different formats, even as a need to know what is held behind a locked or otherwise closed door, where the protagonist is compelled to know what lies beyond the door, especially if there is a sense that what lies beyond the door is something that awaits them, something that they 'must have'.

Within this criminal mindset, there are very few obstacles that can or will sway the perpetrator from obtaining exactly what it is that their mind envies.

In 1989 Nicolas' parents had separated. As a result, Nicolas' mother began a relationship with a younger man. Nicolas remained with his father in the family home while his mother moved into an apartment with her new partner, in the Quartier Pigalle.

Sitting in between the 9th and 18th districts of the city, Pigalle is infamous as one of the most thriving centres for prostitution throughout Europe. The area is actually regarded as one of the most vibrant and thriving red-light districts in the entire world, more so even than the infamous Amsterdam area. The Pigalle is further famed for its Moulin Rouge cabaret theatre, which would inspire the now-famous musical film of the same name in 2001, not to mention the countless reproductions brought to stages throughout the world.

At this time Nicolas would continue to engage his interest in true crime, especially owing to the fact that, in January 1989, the execution of Ted Bundy was about to take place at Florida State Prison. Like most countries at the time, France's media seemed to be dominated by the Ted Bundy case and his impending execution. The television news channels were full of images from Florida showing people who had gathered around the prison, wielding banners such as 'Burn Bundy Burn' and 'Meet Old Sparky' – in reference to the form of execution, the electric chair.

The descriptions of Bundy's crimes themselves seemed to spark interest within Nicolas. With the case being current and high profile, there seemed to be many publications about the case in mainstream book stores, which made for easier accessibility in terms of research, as opposed to the underground book stores which Nicolas had relied on previously to obtain information. The British bookshop chain W H Smith had a store in Paris; in there, Nicolas was able to obtain books and magazines to further his quest for knowledge.

It was the Ted Bundy case where Nicolas first began to gain an interest in more recent true crime perpetrators, as opposed to that of serial killers of a time now passed, such as Jack the Ripper. Whereas the Jack the Ripper case had been fascinating to Nicolas, the new and up-to-date case of Ted Bundy seemed to hold a still greater appeal. It was here where Nicolas was able to lay a foundation for his interests in current crimes, and build up his collection of more active true crime perpetrators such as John Wayne Gacy, and the convicted murderer Henry Lee Lucas, who had at one point confessed to the murder of over 100 people, despite having been only convicted of 11 murders in total.

One recent serial killer who interested Nicolas was the so-called 'Night Stalker', Richard Ramirez, who was on death row at the time. (A book of his life would be released in 1996, using his nickname as its title.) Nicolas was able to find references in book stores to Ramirez's crimes of rape and murder. Not only was Nicolas drawn to the story of his case and life, but in addition – not unlike the Issei Sagawa photos that Nicolas had seen in his uncle's edition of the banned copy of *PHOTO* magazine – Nicolas was drawn to the photographs that he would find in the books. However, unlike the pictures he witnessed of Sagawa's victim, the photos he found regarding the Ramirez case tended to show the crime scenes rather than depictions of the victims. Nicolas' fascination meant that he wanted to see more: more of the victims, more of the in-depth detail. However, as there was no internet to speak of at the time, all that Nicolas had for reference were the books that he could find.

Further to this, Nicolas was beginning to mature physically, and therefore began discovering feelings and emotions regarding his sexuality. Because his parents had separated from each other, Nicolas was dividing his time between his father's apartment in the wealthy 15th District, and his mother's new apartment with her younger companion in Pigalle. The time Nicolas spent in Pigalle made it quite easy for him to visit sex shops and access pornographic material there. It was from these visits that Nicolas discovered his interest in what is known as BDSM (Bondage–Discipline, Dominance–Submission, Sadism–Masochism). However, as Nicolas' love for extreme material continued to develop, it became the case that he could not find suitable, or extreme enough material to satisfy his ever-growing needs.

Nicolas' interests had developed beyond what was considered mainstream, so much in fact that he had to actively go searching in order to find this material, or as Nicolas puts it, 'go cruising' for magazines and videos which suited his needs. The majority of the material that he found seemed to be videos of a female BDSM character, who would beat and dominate the male counterpart in their roles. This was not something that Nicolas wanted to indulge in. In fact, Nicolas wanted to obtain material in where the roles of the BDSM characters were reversed, so that he could witness the male person completely dominate the female. In order to obtain this type of material, Nicolas realised that he would have to 'get his hands dirty', as the majority of this kind of material was considered to be of a sleazy nature – unlike today, where it is readily available on the internet by means of a few clicks of a computer mouse. At the time in Paris, it was an ordeal to obtain the type of material that he wished.

In much in the same manner as when people who were interested in music in the 1980s would find a series of pen-pals, with whom to trade cassette tapes of the latest music worldwide releases, a similar trade was implemented not only for BDSM movies, but also for darker and more extreme horror movies. Locating people to trade with came in the form of advertisements in the series of fanzines and magazines bought from both occult and sex shops. The majority of the trades that would take place via connection through the fanzines were of a much darker nature than the means by which the videos would be bought, even in what was considered to be an underground store.

For example, a person living in the Netherlands, who would have access to material that was censored in France, would be able to connect to a person based in France, and therefore, via mail, trade copies of the censored material. Therefore, via a multitude of letters and mail orders, a person could build their collection other than by what was available to buy in France.

Through this series of trades and communication, Nicolas, at the age of 17, was able to obtain a large amount of the material that he wished in order to satisfy his ever-growing morbid curiosity. In addition to the BDSM material, Nicolas also became aware of what was known in the world of the underground as 'Hate-Zines'. These were a type of fanzine and worked in the same way as most fanzines, where one would find out all of the latest and upcoming news and information about whatever the chosen subject might be. The contrast here, though, was that the hate-zine's content would consist of information about serial killers, both past and present. Examples of hate-zines at this time were *Full Force Frank*, which had notorious issues, and *Boiled Angels*, which comprised topics such as extreme movies, the occult, art, violence... basically, anything that was considered to be underground at the time.

The community which traded in this kind of material was relatively small in number. However, what the community lacked in numbers, it made up for in terms of volume of dark material. The hate-zine *Full Force Frank* would come under investigation by the FBI at a later date, owing to the fact that the owner of the magazine would not only exploit dark material, but at one point gave information about a large arsenal of weapons that he had stored; in addition, the zine seemingly gave instructions on how to commit mass murder and get away with it.

At the time, through the hate-zines and through mail, this was the only way the people who harboured these types of interests could communicate. Nicolas found that by being involved in this small but intimate community, he could obtain a great deal of information regarding his sexual interests in BDSM, as well as his interest in the world of macabre horror and true crime. The one thing that Nicolas wanted to obtain was a snuff movie. The very idea that such films existed hugely excited him. While he had heard stories of such movies, he found that these films were nothing more than an urban legend. The movies calling themselves snuff movies that he had seen, were in fact poorly acted-out portrayals of deaths and proved to be nothing more than deception. There were, of course, rumours that certain serial killers had actually filmed their murders, but this could not be confirmed, as these killers would further incriminate themselves by releasing such films. Therefore, no real evidence of the snuff movies existed.

Because Nicolas had both a fascination with BDSM-centred pornographic material and an ever-growing interest in horror and true crime, it was not surprising to him that the two subjects began to intermingle in his mind. He strongly connected his sexual desires with horror and violence. Although Nicolas was always actively looking for new and fresh material in connection to both of these subjects, by now Nicolas was fully aware of what he wanted in terms of sexual intercourse. He understood that his desires would not be what would be considered to be normal; however, Nicolas was OK with that, and had therefore accepted who he was as a person. All of his fantasies had almost become interlinked, so much so that even his previous fantasies of killing his classmates had now become sexualised in nature.

It is said that pornographic material is a common denominator for serial killers or even sexual sadists. Ted Bundy stated in a now-famous interview that the influence of pornographic material had a large bearing on his life. It was said that the American serial killer Harvey Glatman would pose as a photographer, looking for models to take photos of for magazines. Instead of taking their photos as promised, he would take models back to his apartment and murder them. Even Richard Ramirez, who was largely influenced by the Jack the Ripper killings, was also influenced by pornographic material.

However, Bundy admitted to fellow inmates on death row that it was the images and visions of his killings that actually aroused him, and that these images of death were what was Bundy considered to be *his* pornographic stimulants, rather than pornography itself. Indeed, it was said that Bundy chose to cite the influence of pornography in his murders as a way of manipulating the authorities and gaining a stay of execution, in order to avoid the electric chair. In a sense, he was telling the authorities what they wanted to hear, rather than revealing what Bundy himself found to be sexually stimulating.

It was all of these subjects that Nicolas found himself being drawn to: the convicted killers themselves, the influence of pornography, as well as the nature of the material and videos which he collected from constant correspondence with like-minded people via the fanzines.

The local people he had to engage with on a daily basis, primarily consisting of the students at the school he attended, still continued to see Nicolas as an outcast, and therefore a person to avoid. In particular, there was one girl in his class who gave him a difficult time; naturally, this made Nicolas not particularly like the girl. Therefore, as a means to serve as a revenge for her taunts and attitude towards him, he decided to bring a dead mouse to school, and subsequently placed the dead mouse in the girl's school bag without her knowledge. Upon discovery of the dead mouse, the girl's natural reaction was to be horrified at what she had discovered.

Following the incident in which the young girl discovered the mouse inside her school bag, and once she had subsequently calmed down after her initial fright, it was not long before the insults in the direction of Nicolas resumed, albeit in the form of rumours as opposed to direct taunting. The young girl began a rumour that Nicolas had placed several live mice in a blender to watch the mice die. That rumour seemed to produce even more rumours from other students at the school, each more extreme than the next. As to which of the rumours were in fact true and which had no truth whatsoever, we will never know. Nicolas did nothing to disprove any of the rumours, whether they were true or not: the simple fact was that he simply did not care what the other students were saying about him. Nicolas did, however, seem to enjoy the notoriety which the rumours seemed to bring him in terms of reputation. As a result, Nicolas decided to start bringing a meat cleaver to school, primarily for effect, but also because he found the student's reactions to be funny to him. As a result, Nicolas carried the meat cleaver with him all of the time while at school.

In the summer of 1989, when the school term had been completed, Nicolas went to visit his uncle – the same uncle who owned the Issei Sagawa *PHOTO* magazine – who was renovating a holiday home in Central France. Nicolas travelled with his uncle to the holiday home, where he would assist in the work that needed to be done. The house was located in a small village near the city of Vichy, some 350 kilometres south of Paris. There was rather of lot of work to be done to the Holiday home, and therefore, Nicolas was going to be spending the entirety of his school holiday time in the small village near Vichy.

The neighbouring house, which also happened to be a holiday home, was occupied by a woman from the Netherlands, who had brought her daughter on holiday with her to the small French village. As Nicolas was the only other person in the surrounding area who could speak English, he would be asked to come over to the duo from the Netherlands house, to have a couple of beers in the evening. To which Nicolas obliged. As it turns out, the mother of the girl was attracted to Nicolas, but Nicolas was not attracted to her. However, he was actually interested in the woman's daughter and left with her to go for a stroll through the fields and woods in order to evade the mother's advances.

Nicolas and the young girl, while walking through the field, stopped for a moment and began to kiss one another. The couple got carried away with what they were doing, and soon things progressed to the point where they would have sex. This was the first time that Nicolas had sexual intercourse. The couple lay down and began to have sex: midway through this, Nicolas found himself seeing images of death and torture in his mind, and as a result, he proceeded to raise his hands up to the girl's throat, in order to strangle her. She was unable to breathe, so naturally her face began to change colour. Nicolas was in a state of a trance at this point, more fascinated by the changes in the colours of the skin and breathing of the girl than the event itself. It was then that Nicolas came around from his trance-like state and released the pressure from the girl's neck.

They had stopped what they were doing, and despite having been in complete fear for her life, the girl forgave Nicolas for trying to strangle her. As a result, the girl did not report to anyone in authority, including her mother, what had just happened between the two of them, partly because she did not wish to get into trouble with her mother but also, in fact, because she was very frightened by what had happened. Nicolas had realised that he had hurt the girl by attempting to strangle her, but in what was his first sexual experience, he was more fascinated by the changes in the colour of her skin and her breathing difficulties.

As time progressed over the summer, Nicolas began dating another girl in the area. Rather than continue where he had left off and attempt to strangle the new girl he was dating, he chose to experience a normal sexual education with her. The girl from the Netherlands, although still his neighbour for the duration of the summer, avoided him as best she could. Despite the fact that she was avoiding Nicolas, and even though he was actually dating someone new, he could not get the images of the strangulation from out of his mind. So much so, that he began to fantasise even more about actually killing the girl from the Netherlands.

Nicolas returned to Paris from Vichy and began the new school year. It was here that Nicolas discovered music for the first time. Naturally, he had heard music before, but it was only now that he took particular notice of it. This was when he was 17, which would usually be considered to be late to discover one's musical tastes. It was at this point that he discovered the world of heavy metal music. As with horror and true crime, the world of this music involved tape trading amongst friends, although in this case Nicolas did not need to rely on corresponding with people from other countries to build his collection of musical albums. He would trade tapes with local people, focusing on bands such as Anthrax and Slayer. Nicolas fell in love with the dark and Satanic imagery portrayed on the albums' covers. It was not an avenue which Nicolas had paid too much attention to in the past, but he was now fascinated not only by the music but by the artwork of the albums themselves.

One band in particular that held a fascination for him was Carcass, from Liverpool. The sister of one of the band members was actually studying to be a nurse; her brother had seen her study material, which contained medical pictures of autopsies and body parts for research relating to her studies, and then decided that, instead of using traditional illustrations for the covers of their albums, they would make collages of various medical-related autopsy pictures. A very controversial subject indeed, but nevertheless, artwork that would certainly garner the band's attention.

Nicolas was fascinated by the album covers of the band Carcass, and in turn, through research of this band, was able to discover still more bands of an extreme nature, one of which was the American death metal band Morbid Angel. Not only did Nicolas want to know more about these bands, he also wanted to begin collecting the shirts of these bands, so that he could display album covers and other band-related imagery for himself.

The very first time that Nicolas was able to travel out of France on his own, he decided to go to London. Not only was Nicolas able to purchase his very first music shirt from Tower Records – of the band Slayer – he was able to experience many new things that he had as yet not had the freedom to explore for himself.

The short vacation to London was a completely new experience for Nicolas. The fact that he had travelled there on his own, at the age of 17, meant that he could visit places that he found interesting, without the need for explanations. He was able to visit places such as the London Dungeon – this was at a time when there were actual portrayals of the instruments of torture of old, as opposed to the spectacle that the Dungeon has become these days, where it has apparently taken on a varying, story-themed production of actors, with the emphasis being more like a theatre production than a display of what the dungeons were actually like in historic times. A further place of interest to Nicolas was the famous Madame Tussaud's wax museum. At the time, the museum had on display figures such as characters from film and history that Nicolas had an interest in, with even a character from the *Texas Chainsaw Massacre* being on display. (Once again, the displays of 1989 were somewhat different from what would be found in this famous museum today.)

Another place that Nicolas was able to explore on his own was the famous Highgate cemetery. In folklore, Highgate cemetery was known to have been the resting place and subsequent haunting grounds of the Highgate Vampire, who had been popularised by Lord Sean Manchester. A self-proclaimed 'Vampire Hunter' in the 1970s, Lord Manchester includes depictions of himself apparently driving a stake through a vampire's heart in his book *The Highgate Vampire*.

The Highgate cemetery itself held a great deal of fascination for Nicolas, as the cemetery had a large number of murals, with some seeming to be of the Satanic variety. Nicolas would climb the walls of the cemetery at night, and actually spend the night within the grounds, so as to take in the atmosphere. Spending the entire night in the cemetery had an overwhelming effect on Nicolas. Whereas a great number of people would find the atmosphere of such a place to be daunting at night, Nicolas, in his own words, 'loved it' and, as such, felt completely at home within the grounds.

After his short vacation to London, Nicolas returned home to Paris with his new shirt of the band Slayer as a cherished souvenir. The Satanic imagery of the shirt appealed to Nicolas, and as a result, Nicolas wore it with pride. One occasion when he wore his new shirt was to a film festival in Paris called the 'Festival du film fantastique', whose themes were horror and sci-fi films. Countless numbers of fans of both genres would gather to see what spectacles were on display and take in the trailers and entertainment available to the fans.

At the festival, Nicolas was without a ticket for the event, and as such was standing on the outskirts of the masses of people who were in line, waiting to enter the festival. A man who had a spare ticket for the event saw Nicolas, dressed in his Slayer shirt, and subsequently approached him. The man was also a Slayer fan, and therefore offered his spare ticket to Nicolas. At the time, Nicolas did not know many people who were interested in the same music as he was, and as a result of this chance meeting, a friendship arose. The man was playing a heavy metal band, and therefore had a wide social circle. It was through this man, and his wide circle of friends, that Nicolas was able to interact with what would be his first-ever group of friends.

Nicolas, with his newly acquired friends, would go to places such as record stores, and buy things such as music CDs and VHS tapes, and in turn they would hang out together watching horror movies and listening to music. His new group of friends were also what is known as 'stoners': in other words, they would smoke a lot of marijuana. Nicolas, with the exception of having an odd beer while spending time with his uncle in Vichy, had never really been exposed to drink and drugs, and therefore this was to be yet another new experience for him. Nicolas tried to smoke marijuana, but in truth, he did not like the taste or the smell of it. However, as he was trying to fit in with his new set of friends, he obliged.

The summer of 1989 was spent mainly with his new friends, where they would continue to listen to music and watch horror films together. He had made some connection with the friends in his new group, but there still appeared to be evident gaps between them. Whereas both Nicolas and the group of friends liked the same music, the group seemed to be interested in the dark imagery associated with the bands only as a form of entertainment. It also seemed as if they had a different belief system from what Nicolas had. The imagery in the music and films they enjoyed was related to death and dismemberment, and unlike the rest of the group, Nicolas had a genuine interest in these subjects. When he spoke of these subjects with obvious fascination, the members of the group would appear to be shocked and even disgusted at times, while, in truth, Nicolas was not. As a result, therefore, the gap between Nicolas and the group seemed to widen even further. There were some common interests; however, not enough to have that much in common.

The summer drew to an end, and it was time for Nicolas to return to school for the beginning of the new term. It seemed that once again, Nicolas found himself in a state of isolation when outside of the school day. Nicolas was not actually that bothered by this turn of events, as it allowed him to spend his free time in the grounds of cemeteries: a practice that Nicolas had always felt comfortable with and enjoyed greatly. In his spare time after the school day had ended, Nicolas found himself frequenting cemeteries up to two or three afternoons each week.

In Paris, indeed in the whole of France, a family will not only purchase a burial plot but will pay 'rent' on the plot for many years to come. After the agreed number of years have passed, and the surviving members of any particular family have either moved on or become deceased themselves, the state will exhume the remains of a burial plot and have them incinerated, thus freeing the burial plot for use by another family.

On one afternoon, Nicolas was passing through the Passy cemetery; as he walked past a small mausoleum, he noticed that the entrance door had been left open. Workers had been in the process of exhuming the old graves inside the mausoleum but were now on a break and had left the door to the mausoleum open in error.

Nicolas decided that he would take a look inside the building. Inside, he noticed that all of the bones had been exhumed from the graves and placed in garbage bags, which would be gathered up and sent for incineration. There were four bags of bones in total. Nicolas was not about to pass on such an opportunity to gather human remains, which would further feed his morbid fascinations. Unable to physically carry all four bags, Nicolas managed to gather the two largest of the bags of human remains.

A bag in each of his hands, Nicolas proceeded to leave the cemetery, and make his way towards his home. As he passed through the streets of Paris, onlookers would look in disbelief at Nicolas and his collection of bones. The bags had been filled by the workers in a careless fashion, which meant that sections of the garbage bags had been torn in places, so that human bones were protruding from the torn bags. Nicolas made his way towards the subway train that he travelled on to reach his home destination. As Nicolas took his seat on the subway, he began to rummage through the bags, in order to see what specific bones he had been lucky enough to have found. Such was his elation at his discovery that he did not notice the foul smell which escaped from one of the bags as he opened it. On the adjacent seat to Nicolas on the subway was an African woman who had unmistakably noticed the smell emanating from the open bag of bones; as such, her focus was directed entirely towards what it was that Nicolas was doing. Nicolas did not notice the attention of the African woman at first, and it was only when he removed one of the bones from the bag that he noticed the sheer look of horror on the the that of the woman's face.

In truth, Nicolas did not care for the reactions of others regarding his newly acquired collection of human remains. He felt as though discovering these bones was his life's destiny to this point. He felt as though as he had been on something like the shopping experience of his life, and he was beyond excited with his acquisitions. What he was aware of, however, was the amount of attention that he was seemingly attracting to himself. Thankfully for Nicolas, he managed to reach his home with the remains without being apprehended. Once there, Nicolas decorated his bedroom with the collection of skulls and bones that he had acquired.

The attention that the bag of human remains brought in his direction was not the only attention that Nicolas was drawing towards himself at that time. At the time, there had been a mass shooting at a school in Montreal, Canada, where a gunman named Marc Lépine had entered the school grounds, held a group of students at gunpoint, then proceeded to separate the girls from the boys. He then opened fire on the group of girls.

This was of course in no way connected to Nicolas, especially since the shooting had taken place in another country. However, the headmaster of Nicolas' school, having seen the shooting on the news, coupled with the rumours that had been circulating about Nicolas in the school – of having carried knives and meat cleavers to school, as well as placing dead animals in the school bags of other students – decided to call Nicolas to his office for a meeting, in an attempt to avoid a similar event taking place on his own school grounds. Nicolas' father was also required to attend the meeting. The headmaster explained his concerns to both Nicolas and his father, and once again it was suggested that Nicolas should be sent to see a therapist for what was deemed to be his peculiar behaviour.

As with the previous suggestions about Nicolas attending

therapy, Nicolas' father was in denial as to the seriousness of his son's behaviour. As result, he decided to not take any action following the headmaster's advice. This sequence of events, though, did alert Nicolas further still to the attention that he was drawing towards himself. He therefore understood that, in order to remain under the radar as such, he would have to start being more careful about carrying knives at places such as school. Nicolas understood that boasting about carrying knives as he had previously done would almost certainly draw unwanted attention to himself. This would, in turn, result in his actions being more closely monitored. Close monitoring of his behaviour could have a detrimental impact on the freedom to be able to visit graveyards and gain access to burial chambers.

It was at this point that Nicolas had an epiphany. He wished to be able to feed his insatiable and growing envy of what the world of the dead contained for him but knew that his fascinations were leading him to behaviour that was deemed to be not only taboo, but actively criminal. This realisation did nothing to ease his growing obsession for the macabre. Instead, it just made Nicolas aware that he had to be careful not to be caught, so that he could go on indulging his morbid fascinations.

FIVE

FEEDING LIFE THROUGH THE DEATH OF OTHERS

THE AGHORI, OR Aghora, are comprised of a small sect of people in India who are devout followers of Shiva. This is often considered to be contradictory to orthodox Hinduism.

The Aghori will often smear their bodies in the cremation ashes of human corpses, and construct spiritual jewellery from the bones of human remains. They believe that everything that exists in life must be perfect and that to dent the perfection of anything would be to deny the sacredness of all life in its manifestation, and that doing so would be a denial of the supreme being.

Therefore, embracing all things, including what would be considered as negative in Western society, is deemed by the Aghori to be a means for one's self-realisation with the absolute, or supreme being. The Aghori maintain that all negative aspects are illusory: things such as pollution and taboos are not seen as negative concepts, as they are all borne of the same spiritual source. Feelings such as shame, anger, lust, greed, obsession or hatred are deemed to be aspects of the eight great bonds, or nooses. The Aghori's practice is centred around the spiritual removal of the bonds, so that the soul of the individual can truly be free: free to indulge in life and death without negative concepts such as shame.

Therefore, embracing things such as death, and the use of human remains as a means in which to invoke a full and spiritual life, is a fundamental key to one's self-realisation with all things being perfection. To hold a sense of shame pertaining to modern taboos would be a denial of one's true self and worth.

———————————————————————

At the beginning of 1990, Nicolas, despite having drawn attention to himself as a result of his behaviour at school – attention owing to the recent massacre at a Canadian school, to which he had no connection – nonetheless decided to frequent the local cemeteries of Paris. However, he did so under the cover of darkness, and further disguised his appearance by wearing a mask. On one particular night, he attempted to gain entrance to the Pierre Garnier cemetery in Boulogne Billancourt, located in the west of Paris. The gates to the grounds were locked, and the walls that secured the cemetery were approximately two metres in height. There was, however, a car park on the perimeter of the grounds, where Nicolas would be able to gain access to the graveyard.

Prior to his night-time mission, Nicolas had done research on the cemetery by scouting the grounds during the day. There he had seen that a fresh burial site had been constructed and covered in nothing more than a corrugated metal sheet, as the entire process of the burial had not yet been completed. Nicolas, armed with this knowledge – and equipped with black camouflage attire, military-style shovel, gloves, rope and a small tool kit, including a large screwdriver – climbed over the walls of the cemetery, and made his way to the fresh grave that he had remembered from his daylight visit to the grounds. It was February, and therefore winter in Paris, and the cold and murky skies assisted as a perfect cover for Nicolas to indulge his interests.

Once Nicolas had scaled the walls of the cemetery, he felt a sudden rush of energy. It was as though he felt a sense of home-coming. As a result of these feelings, Nicolas felt as though he was the master of his own realm. He made his way to the fresh burial plot without so much as an upwards glance, as though he was being subconsciously driven to the spot in which the fresh grave was located. Once he arrived at the burial site, Nicolas removed the corrugated metal sheet covering the fresh grave to access what lay beneath. Nicolas took care not to make any loud noises in doing so, as he did not wish to alert anyone as to his whereabouts or draw unnecessary attention to what he was doing.

Underneath the metal sheet was a burial coffin. On either side of the coffin was a small amount of space into which Nicolas concluded that he would be able to manoeuvre himself. He climbed down next to the coffin. The coffin itself was placed upon wooden planks and, to Nicolas' surprise, was buried only about one and a half metres deep into the ground. He was unable to see exactly what it was that lay underneath the coffin, but he estimated that it was in fact, more coffins: it was common at the time for burial plots to contain multiple layers of coffins, stacked one on top of the other.

Nicolas examined the coffin directly in front of him. He noticed that the plaque on the coffin was inscribed with what he deemed to be Chinese symbols. He therefore deduced that the person inside the coffin was of Asian origin. The coffin itself appeared to be new and made of oak. Without being able to make an accurate estima-tion, Nicolas presumed that the weight of the coffin, with the body inside, was approximately 100 kilograms. There were eight screws in the lid of the coffin which held the coffin closed. After checking to see that there was no one else around to disturb him, Nicolas began to loosen the screws. Once he had removed all of the screws, he carefully removed the lid and opened the coffin. In order not to lose his screwdriver, he wedged it into the now displaced coffin lid. What was revealed to him was the body of an elderly Asian woman, who had, in Nicolas' estimation, been dead for no more than one month at the most. Nicolas was trembling with excitement; his palms had begun to sweat with anticipation, and at this point any thoughts of consequences for his actions were the furthest thing from his mind. It was almost as though Nicolas was in a trance, with his sole focus on the deceased Asian woman in front of him. As he had opened the coffin, gas was emitted from inside. The gas smelled foul, but in truth, Nicolas had been expecting any smells that he might encounter from inside of the coffin to be far worse than this. Therefore, this was a positive aspect of surprise.

Nicolas closed his eyes for a moment, as though to take in what was happening before him, and when he opened his eyes, there was the deceased Asian woman in front of him. All things considered, the corpse was in good condition. Her eyes looked sunken, her mouth was slightly open, and it was almost as though her skin had been coated in a wax-like substance, preserving her features. In Nicolas' recollection some time later, the deceased woman looked peaceful. She was wearing a white shirt, and on the white shirt, in what appeared to be the mid-section of the body near the ribcage, there was a green stain. It was from this area of the body that the foul smell was being emitted into the air.

Nicolas took the screwdriver from the lid of the coffin and proceeded to touch the deceased woman's skin with the tip of the screwdriver. Nicolas was curious as to whether the woman's skin was going to feel hard or soft, as to gain an understanding as to its overall consistency. Nicolas then placed the screwdriver into the woman's mouth, between the lips, and began to push the screwdriver around. This was more a means to test and observe what the state of the woman's body was like. Nicolas tried to manoeuvre the screwdriver around the woman's mouth but owing to his position on the planks which held up the coffin, Nicolas was unable to gain the leverage to do so.

Nicolas was apprehensive about using his hands to touch the

woman's skin at this point, and therefore continued to experiment with the deceased woman's body using the tip of the screwdriver. There was absolutely nothing sexual in nature of Nicolas' touching of the body; it was more experimental, akin to a cat playing with a dead mouse. Nicolas was also curious whether the woman still had blood flowing inside her body, so he decided to stab the body with the screwdriver, softly at first, and then harder so that he was able to break the skin. When he removed the screwdriver from the body, Nicolas noticed that there was no blood or even liquid on the surface of the screwdriver whatsoever. He did not do this violently, but more in what could be deemed an investigative way.

After roughly half an hour inside of the burial plot, Nicolas heard a noise in the background. As a result, he woke from his trance-like state and decided that it be best to leave the plot. He took a Polaroid of the woman's body and then carefully placed the lid back on the coffin, reinstating the screws which had held the lid in place.

As this was the first time that Nicolas had done anything of this nature, he felt as though he has broken new ground in terms of self-discovery. The fact that he was able to gain access to the grave so easily filled Nicolas with a form of energy that he was unable to describe. He felt empowered, almost as though the graveyard belonged to him. The practice of opening the grave did not feel like grave robbery to Nicolas, as it was an event in which he made observations more than anything else. In fact, more than the Polaroid, what Nicolas felt he took from the burial site was more of a spiritual keepsake, in that he was enlightening his exploration of death; the body itself was insignificant, as this was more of a personal experience to Nicolas, fulfilling his need to fuel his compulsions.

For the days and weeks that followed, Nicolas checked the newspapers and media for any reports of the desecration of this grave. There were none. As a result of this, Nicolas felt as though he were protected. More specifically, he felt as though he was being protected by the demon Pazuzu. A short time later, Nicolas visited the Pazuzu statue at the Louvre Museum, and subsequently meditated in front of the statue. In doing so, Nicolas felt a further surge of energy, energy which made him feel even safer and further connected to Pazuzu, to the point that he felt as though he had the energy and ability to do anything. Anything at all.

Following this, Nicolas would still continue to visit graveyards, but his activities were affected by an incident in May of 1990: a body from a Jewish cemetery in the south of France had been moved from its burial site and then mutilated. The incident served to create a media frenzy, giving the impression that desecrations like this were related to hate crimes. Certain sectors of the media even went as far as to suggest that such desecrations were connected to black masses. Even the French President at the time, François Mitterrand, made a television appearance, condemning the desecrations. As a result, a consistent police presence was to be seen at cemeteries all over France, in order to prevent further desecrations from taking place. One day, as Nicolas was walking through a cemetery in Paris, he was approached by two policemen, who decided to stop him and search his bag. The policemen discovered a screwdriver in his bag, but for some reason decided to let him go without further investigation. This served to make Nicolas realise that he would need to be more careful about visiting cemeteries, and as a result, Nicolas eased his exploration of death for a short period of time.

The reduction of Nicolas' activities in the cemeteries gave rise to him once again making attempts to bolster some form of an active social life. As a result of this, Nicolas began dating a Filipino girl who was studying in the west of Paris at the time.

The relationship was short-lived, but Nicolas began dating several of the girl's friends. All of these relationships were no more than fleeting, as Nicolas felt as though he had no connection to the girls and therefore derived no form of satisfaction from his interactions with them. At the same time, Nicolas' father's health was deteriorating following a seizure brought on by a bout of heavy drinking and smoking, and this, coupled with the fact that Nicolas' bedroom was filled with human remains, meant that he never brought any of the girls back to his own house.

The subsequent reactivation of Nicolas' diminishing social life brought with it a re-acquaintance with his long-standing friend, Stephen, whom he had met at the horror and sci-fi film festival on his return from London. Stephen introduced Nicolas to even more hardcore versions of extreme music, including a kind of electronic music known as powernoise, which was employed by bands such as Whitehouse. As Stephen was well connected socially within the music scene, the combination of a love of heavy metal and the macabre set the tone for how Nicolas would dress. He began to resemble the character from the *Reanimator* movies, complete with the black and white garments that the character wore. It was a sense of dress that made Nicolas look like a pall-bearer. However, the *Reanimator* dress sense would not last forever, and soon it gave way to Nicolas' new interest in training his body.

Nicolas began to work out. He bought himself a set of dumbbells and a weight training bench, and it was not long before he began to obtain good results. The more Nicolas trained, the less he looked like a skinny teenager. Nicolas, in his own words, describes himself as beginning to look like a 'young soldier of Satan'. The interest in working out gave rise to an interest in sports, and as a result, his dress sense began to take on a more stylish look, more casual than the macabre outfits that he had previously worn.

The process of getting fit was not done with the purpose of gaining female attraction, but more so with the idea of gaining greater mental strength. Nicolas also reasoned that if he was fitter in body, then he would become more proficient at climbing walls and breaking into cemeteries.

While Nicolas was training his body, he was also continuing to trade video tapes by use of the hate-zines that he had been active with previously. His searches were dominated by the desire to obtain more S&M tapes to add to his collection and included videos depicting real-life torture such as *Shocking Asia*, a film that was subsequently banned in Finland due to its graphic content. Another type of graphically violent film that he searched for involved ritualistic torture, which of course were not readily available in mainstream media. These searches provided a temporary distraction for Nicolas while he was unable to frequent cemeteries and therefore had to find alternative means by which to satisfy his compulsion with death and the macabre. Further to this, for Nicolas' visual appreciation, he began to collect movie posters of films that he deemed to be macabre.

Nicolas collected movie posters such as films called *Necromantik* (1987) and *Cannibal Holocaust* (1980) – the latter being the Japanese version of the movie poster which depicts an impaled woman – as well as posters from the film *Henry: Portrait of a Serial Killer* (1986). Further to this, Nicolas once again furthered his interest in true crime stories, such as the Hong Kong film *Men behind the Sun* (1988), centred around the graphic depiction of the biological weapon experiments performed by the Japanese during World War Two.

All of Nicolas' interests fed into his morbid obsessions with death, and as a result, these morbid obsessions began to coincide with his fantasies once again. Nicolas would fantasise about dating girls and disembowelling them, to the point that during sexual intercourse, he was unable to climax unless he conjured up these images of disembowelment within his mind. To

Nicolas at 18, wearing a Henry: Portrait of a Serial Killer *T-shirt.*

use Nicolas' own description, this would be in the same way that another man would fantasise about a beautiful girl in order to climax during sexual intercourse with a less attractive girl.

At the beginning of the summer of 1990, Nicolas went to New York with his father for three weeks, as part of yet another excursion that his father was undertaking in his role for his banking firm. The bank that his father worked for had a branch on New York's Wall Street, and as a result, he was required to roll out the banking network for the New York branch. This would be the furthest that Nicolas would have travelled from France up until this point.

New York was unlike anything Nicolas had ever seen up until that point. The size of the skyscrapers was so impressive that for the first two days, Nicolas found himself getting a painful neck from basically just looking upwards. Their hotel was located on 46th Street, and it was located directly opposite the Scientology headquarters in New York. Nicolas deemed the city to be 'wild', a trait Nicolas found to be impressive. The streets were filled with what Nicolas refers to as 'crazy street preachers' and also 'gang bangers'. He also recalls seeing people who were very heavily tattooed. The number of homeless people that he saw was extremely overwhelming; Nicolas also mentions that for the first time in his life he got to see a mounted policeman actually travel on horseback into the subway section of the local railway. It was like nothing that Nicolas had ever encountered in his life before, and certainly far different from anything that he had witnessed in Paris up to that point in his life.

At night-time in New York, Nicolas would spend the time with his father frequenting lavish bars, spending time not only with his father, but also with the New York-based bank employees that his father was then working with. These people were younger than Nicolas' father, yet they seemed to be intrigued by the pair, partially due to the fact that they both had French accents. The duo thus received a lot of attention from not only Nicolas' father's work colleagues, but also from any people who happened to be in the bars at the time. One of the bars or clubs that they attended was the Tunnel Bar, now closed, which was in the Chelsea region of New York. (The bar was once owned by Michael Alig, who served time in prison for a murder pertaining to an alleged drug debt in the mid-1990s.)

The standard depiction of Baphomet,
from Dogme et Rituel de la Haute Magie *(1856) by Eliphas Levi*

The club itself was comprised of what Nicolas described as 'Yuppies', with girls suspended in cages and an extraordinary number of drag queens in attendance. Nicolas' father would become so intoxicated that Nicolas was forced to get a cab home. This was Nicolas' first experience of being in a nightclub. The truth is that, owing to the atmosphere and the clientele of the club,

Nicolas once again felt as though he did not fit in with the club-goers, and as a result Nicolas did not find the experience fun.

Instead of frequenting clubs that he could not connect with, Nicolas decided to venture out and discover what New York had to offer in terms of occult material. Nicolas discovered an occult store in the Chelsea region of New York: unlike the occult stores in Paris, in where the stores sold only books, this store sold every manner of occult material that Nicolas could only have dreamed of prior to this point. The store was called The Magickal Childe. As Nicolas entered the store, he saw a giant statue of the Baphomet deity, and immediately knew that he was in a place where he would be comfortable. Behind the counter was a large, bearded man, who appeared to be observing Nicolas as he wandered through the store. The man turned out to be the owner of the store, none other than Herman Slater, an author and editor who was responsible for books such as the *Introduction to Witchcraft*, the *Hoodoo Bible* and several versions of the Pagan Ritual. Prior to his death in 1992, Slater was renowned for being an occult high priest of the Wicca religion.

As Nicolas wandered through the store, Herman Slater continued to observe Nicolas, as well as three 'Goth Girls' who had been paying close attention to Nicolas as he perused the store. Nicolas heard the three girls whispering and giggling but continued to go about his business. Nicolas picked up a copy of Anton LaVey's *The Satanic Bible* and took it to the counter where Slater was sitting. Slater and the three girls were surprised when they heard Nicolas speak with a French accent. One of the girls, who Nicolas came to know by her 'goth' name of 'Cassandra', was more than a little intrigued by Nicolas. After purchasing the book, Nicolas engaged in further conversation with Cassandra and suggested that the pair go to the corner bar to talk further.

Cassandra – whose real name, Nicolas came to learn, was Bev – was intrigued by Nicolas, and his tales of the cemeteries of Paris, as well as the Catacombs there. As a result, she hung on every word that Nicolas was saying. The pair decided to date each other for the duration of the time that Nicolas would spend in New York. Nicolas had a lot of cash from his father, but instead of spending the money on tourist excursions, Nicolas decided that he would use it to spend time with Bev.

This was the first time that Nicolas had dated a goth girl, and he found it a completely different experience from anything that he had encountered previously. Bev's grandfather was a diabetic, and as a result of this, she had access to his blood lancets which her grandfather used to test glucose levels in his blood. Having obtained these lancets, she and Nicolas would engage in blood play. They would draw blood from each other and taste their partner's blood. Nicolas loved this blood play and took in as much of Bev's blood as he possibly could. The sensation was even better than when he had tasted his own blood. The blood of someone else seemed to give him more energy. The sensation of drinking Bev's blood was a mixture of both sexual and spiritual emotions, as the pain that he was causing her was enjoyed by both parties with what seemed like sadistic intent. Despite the sirens that wailed outside on the streets of New York, Nicolas and Bev were oblivious, as if they were both in a trance. The entire experience seemed surreal to both of them.

The pair arranged to meet one last time before Nicolas would have to return to France. However, on the final day, Bev did not arrive for their meeting: she had hinted to Nicolas on previous occasions that she felt depressed about having to say goodbye. Nicolas himself was depressed at the fact that he knew that he would never get to see her again. In the past, he had felt lost, as he had never made a true connection to another human being; now, having made such a strong one with Bev, he felt low, as she was everything that he could have hoped to find in another person.

On Nicolas' return to Paris, he would be entering into what would prove to be his final year both at school and at home living with his father. In the final year of school in France, at the time, students were mandatorily required to study philosophy for the final year. In addition to giving the students a grasp of philosophy, this was considered a method of preparing students for life outside school, a means of social adaptation and a way of fostering a love of the French republic.

The final year in school did not go well for Nicolas. His teacher did not like Nicolas' chosen philosophers, in particular Friedrich Nietzsche, as well as works such as *Might is Right* by Ragnar Redbeard. While this philosophy was personal to Nicolas, it proved to be too much for the teacher. As a result, the teacher not only gave Nicolas bad grades to reflect this, but also publicly shamed him during class, using his studies as a way of ridiculing Nicolas. It was not so much Nicolas' writing that the teacher was publicly mocking, but more the philosophical viewpoints that the teacher was personally opposed to.

Further to Nicolas' issues at school, he discovered that his father's drinking was becoming more and more severe, and as a result his health was failing even further. In addition, Nicolas' father seemed to be attracting the friendship of African men whose sole intention was to extort money out of him and take advantage of his generous nature. Further to this, Nicolas' grandfather on his father's side was deteriorating from Alzheimer's disease. This made Nicolas reminisce about his other grandfather, who had died of a stroke in 1982. Not that this filled Nicolas with any form of sadness, however: given the circumstances, he had expected his grandfather to pass away as well.

At this point, Nicolas' interest in visiting cemeteries was looking more promising. The police presence in cemeteries seemed to be easing up, and as a result, Nicolas found he was able to frequent these grounds with less worry than previously. Therefore, Nicolas started returning to these cemeteries more often. Initially, he did not break into the mausoleums as much as before, as he was quite content with stealing things such as crosses and other religious memorabilia to begin with. At the Père Lachaise cemetery, he was able to break into the main building where the ovens for the cremations were located. There were plaques on the walls, depicting the names associated with some 15,000 cremation urns that were stored behind the plaques. Nicolas found a way of breaking into the area behind the plaques. To his surprise, there were no coffins at all located there, just the cremation urns. He decided to keep some of the urns, and their contents, as souvenirs for himself.

With Bev becoming more a distant memory of what was, rather than what could have been, Nicolas was beginning to understand and accept the fact that he would be forced to lead a lonely life. There were very few people that would not only understand his mindset but engage in his fascinations with him. Therefore, Nicolas put the thought of social interaction to the back of his mind and returned his attention to graves and burial plots.

In the urns that Nicolas had collected from the cemetery, he found not only the cremation ashes, but also bits of bones that had not been fully consumed by the fire. Nicolas made necklaces and jewellery from the bits of bone that he recovered. Further to this, as Nicolas was still using some of his free time to work out and exercise, he decided to add some of the ashes from the urns to the protein shakes that he would drink in order to build muscle. Nicolas was a strong believer in spiritual energy at this point, and he felt as though the consuming of death, by way of the ashes in his milkshakes, was part of his process in the transformation of turning death into life.

Nicolas believed strongly in this philosophy – creating life from death – and his bedroom reflected his belief system. Looking back, Nicolas describes his bedroom sat this time as bizarre-looking. His cupboards were filled with items such as urns and human bones, so much so that he was finding it increasingly difficult to hide these things from his father. There was a basement to the property, and Nicolas decided to secure the basement with his own padlock, and then store the remaining urns and bones there. He even built an altar where he created a statue of the Indian goddess Kali from the remains of human bones that he had collected. It was at this altar in Nicolas' private basement where he strengthened his inner belief that if you are going to die, then you must feed your life on the death of others.

While Nicolas was feeding his own motto in his life, he still had some form of a narrow social life. He would see a small group of friends but would not allow them to know exactly what it was that he was doing with remained of his spare time. Nicolas did attend some concerts with his friends, but while his friends would like going to nightclubs, Nicolas had no interest in this. Therefore he felt as though the social gap was widening once again. Not only this, but even though his friends seemed to be interested in the dark imagery of their favourite music, they still thought that Nicolas would take the concept a little too far, unaware that the dark imagery that interested Nicolas had, in actual fact, very little to do with the music as such. However, Nicolas found it better for his friends to believe that the imagery was related to the music, rather than what his interests were actually rooted in; he understood that revealing the truth to his friends would almost certainly bring him and his activities some unwanted attention.

In 1991, Nicolas was presented with the option of going to University, having finished school that summer. Initially, he had wanted to go to medical school and learn more about the human body. However, his grades did not reach the standard required to attend medical studies. Therefore, as a second option, Nicolas chose to study Psychology. The main issue with the Psychology course was that the classes were approximately 80 per cent female, while the resulting 20 per cent of males in the class were not the sort of people that Nicolas would have chosen to socialise with.

Therefore, just as with every other aspect of Nicolas' life up until that point, he found himself being alienated. Feeling despondent from the outset, Nicolas found himself sitting at the back of the class, and not really paying attention to the lecturer.

The summer of 1991 was the summer of Jeffrey Dahmer. The infamous 'Cannibal of Milwaukee' was appearing on every news media channel, not only in France but worldwide. While everyone that Nicolas spoke to about Dahmer was disgusted at his crimes, Nicolas found that he had an unspoken connection to the convicted murderer. Nicolas would study Dahmer's case in depth, looking at every possible angle from which the case was being presented and making up his own mind.

Nicolas had learned that Dahmer had apparently committed his first murder at the age of 17. As Nicolas was now 18, he mused to himself that he would have to endeavour to catch up to the Milwaukee cannibal. In addition to the Dahmer case, which was everywhere on the media, this was also the same summer when *The Silence of the Lambs* was released in the cinema. Together, these coincidental factors were to give the impression that the year 1991 spawned 'Serial Killer Culture' as a mainstay of the entertainment world, bequeathing us the idea of the serial killer as a modern-day bogeyman.

On the campus of the Jussieu University which Nicolas would be attending, there was a huge tower in the centre of the campus. Nicolas was able to pick the locks of the tower's gates – he had become good at this after picking locks to get into cemeteries – and climbed to the top of the tower, making his way onto the roof of the building. From the top of the tower, Nicolas was able to look down at the students. At the time of the day that he was on the rooftop, it was between classes, and therefore the majority of the students were in the courtyard, either sitting down to take a break or making their way towards their next class. Nicolas thought just how easy it would be to sit on the rooftop and shoot the students at will. It was at this point that Nicolas decided that he was going to obtain a rifle.

In France at this time, it was perfectly legal for a person to buy and own a .22 calibre rifle (0.22 inches or 5.6mm gauge), or even a shotgun of almost any gauge. Nicolas decided to start going to gun shops, investigating the prices of rifles and seeing if there was any way that he could potentially buy a rifle without having to produce identification. At this point, buying a rifle was nothing more than an idea; however, it was a very unusual one, considering that the massacre at Columbine High School in the United States had not yet taken place. Nicolas' thought process was more or less a natural progression from the fantasies that Nicolas had been having with relation to killing his classmates when he was younger; the notable difference, though, was that Nicolas was coming to an age when the prospects of fulfilling his fantasies were more realistic than they had previously been. In truth, Nicolas did not have to give this development of his fantasies a great deal of thought, as the entire progression seemed very straightforward to him at the time.

The fantasies were coupled with the fact that his isolation and alienation from the rest of society had left Nicolas with a feeling of general misanthropy, as well as more specific feelings of hatred and social distance from the rest of the public. So much, in fact, that Nicolas was not even bothering to date girls anymore. Each girl that he met was entirely different from him and his belief system, to the point that it was impossible for Nicolas to make any real connections with them. Therefore, as a result, Nicolas had given up on his attempts to even try and find common ground with potential partners.

Although Nicolas was not able to obtain a rifle straight away, he did carry with him a canister of mace at all times. He did not use the mace on anyone in particular; however, the mace did fall out of his bag during class while in university, and as a result it went off and sprayed the entire classroom with the gas. The mace went everywhere, hurting the eyes of his classmates and burning their throats from inhaling the gas. Nicolas was called to the head of the university. However, unlike the cases in high school where he was called to the headmaster's office, he was not let off with an instruction or suggestion to seek therapy. This time he was expelled from the university. Nicolas did not feel as though he was able to tell his father the news of his expulsion from the university, and instead, got up each morning under the pretence of attending class as normal. However, instead of going to university, Nicolas decided to frequent cemeteries for longer periods of time than he had previously done.

Nicolas would visit the Père Lachaise cemetery on a regular basis, walking around the grounds for hours at a time. This is the cemetery where the legendary rock musician Jim Morrison is buried. Beyond the musician's grave, in an older section of the cemetery, is a section of graves which are in ruin, with broken-down mausoleums and tombstones, quite often with the trunks of trees growing from the broken sections of the graves.

Nicolas found these sections of the cemetery to be fascinating. However, there was a downside to enjoying this rustic section of the ruins, the downside being that the area was quite often frequented by gay men, looking for other gay men to engage with. Nicolas found that on, occasion, he would be followed by one of these men, in the hope that Nicolas was there for the same reason that they were there for. Obviously, however, Nicolas was there for his own reasons. As a precautionary measure, Nicolas would carry with him a ball pein hammer, so that he could defend himself from any advances. He would hide the hammer down the leg of his black camouflaged trousers and grip the hammer tight should he feel that one of the men was about to make an unwelcome advance in Nicolas' direction. On occasion, he found himself having to show the hammer to men who were getting too close to him, as a means of warding off any further advancement.

Père Lachaise cemetery

In addition to Nicolas' visiting of cemeteries, he continued to correspond with people who he had met from the hate-zine magazines. One such magazine where he would correspond was *Answer Me*, which concentrated its focus on the social pathologies that the couple who ran the magazine had an interest in. One person that Nicolas was able to correspond with was the author of the Redneck Manifesto, Jim Goad. Nicolas sent Goad photographs, to which Goad replied with a letter stating that he wished that 'Germany would invade France all over again', having clearly not been impressed by Nicolas' correspondence.

Another group of people who Nicolas corresponded with were Mike Diana of *Boiled Angels* magazine (who became the first person in the United States to be jailed for obscenity) and Randall Phillip of *Fuck* magazine. Nicolas would send these people pieces of bones as well as photographs that he had taken. Nicolas seemed to pick up a certain amount of notoriety from this correspondence, well before any of his better-known activities took place.

Passy cemetery

As 1991 rolled into 1992, Nicolas would visit the Passy cemetery, the cemetery where Nicolas had first broken into mausoleums and where coffins of Russian immigrants were blockaded behind heavy marble slabs inside the crypts. One day, as Nicolas was walking through the Passy cemetery, he decided that this day would be the one where he would gain access to the coffins behind the heavy marble slabs. Nicolas approached a crypt at approximately noon, when he knew that the groundsman would be off having his lunch. As a result, Nicolas would be able to obtain access to a crypt without fear of being detected. Nicolas had picked out a mausoleum which he had deemed to be special to him, and subsequently picked the lock to the mausoleum and gained access. As Nicolas went down the stairs to where the coffins were kept, he noticed that the marble slabs which the coffins were held behind were about waist height, just as they were in the mausoleum that he had first broken into.

Nicolas began by removing the cement which surrounded the

marble slabs. The first slab gave way and came crashing to the ground, almost crushing Nicolas' feet as it fell. Luckily, Nicolas was unharmed, and after a quick check to see that no one had heard the crashing of the marble slab, he returned to his mission of trying to excavate the coffin from the hole in the wall where the slab had been placed.

Nicolas placed both of his hands on the coffin and tried to wedge it towards himself. The coffin was very heavy, and it took an enormous amount of effort to make the coffin move. Nicolas' palms were sweating from the amount of energy that it took to displace the coffin. As he moved the coffin to the edge of the hole in the crypt, the coffin unexpectedly came hurtling towards him. Once again, Nicolas was able to evade the falling item from the wall. Nicolas took one more look at the entrance to the mausoleum, as he had previously, to make sure that no one had heard the sound of the coffin crashing onto the floor. When he was sure it was safe to do so, he returned to the coffin and unscrewed the lid.

The coffin, Nicolas knew, would contain someone Russian. The crypt itself was decorated with pictures of Russian saints and icons. Nicolas had an overwhelming desire to discover what was inside the coffin and looked inside. What he discovered was a zinc coffin. A zinc coffin is generally used for one of three reasons: if the body needed to be transported by plane; if the person had died of an infectious disease; or if the person was in a temporary burial site and would be moved at a later time. Judging by the dates on the plaque on the coffin, Nicolas estimated that this particular coffin had been there for about one year.

Nicolas pried open the zinc coffin. When he did so, he noticed that the body was in an immaculate condition, the zinc having cut off any air supply to the corpse and therefore preserved the body.

Nicolas' intentions were to decapitate the corpse and place the head on the steps of the famous cathedral of Notre Dame, next to the statue of Joan of Arc there. However, in his zeal to get into the mausoleum, Nicolas had forgotten to bring with him a hacksaw that he required to decapitate the body. Therefore, he was forced to abandon his plans; he would need to return to the body later, when it was safe to do so, with the necessary tools required to decapitate the body. In the meantime, exhausted after removing the coffin from the wall, Nicolas was quite content to just sit with the corpse and meditate. He had lit candles inside the mausoleum and simply sat there, taking in all the energy of death that he could. The body itself was covered completely in a shroud; even the head of the corpse was covered. As Nicolas was unable to remove the corpse's head, he had to settle for stabbing the body. He stabbed the body approximately 50 times in total.

Nicolas eventually left the mausoleum. Before he did, he blew out all of the candles in the room, packed his things and then locked the door to the mausoleum behind him.

After almost three months had passed, when Nicolas was certain that no one had been made aware of this break-in, he returned to the body with the sole purpose of decapitating the corpse. The problem was, though, that after three months of fresh air, the body had begun to rot, and as a result of decomposition, the shroud had turned from white to brown. The body itself had become infested with maggots and gave off an extremely foul smell. Nicolas felt like throwing up due to the smell emitted from the corpse. He therefore concluded that he was not going to be able to remove the head of the corpse, and as a result, he decided once again to cover his tracks and head home.

In the time between when Nicolas had first opened the coffin inside the mausoleum and when he returned to decapitate the corpse, Nicolas' friend Stephen had started a record label and had signed a Swedish band called Dissection. At the time the Black Metal scene in Norway was booming; unbeknownst to Nicolas, the scene was fraught with a series of murders, suicides, and church burnings. Nicolas did not care for the music itself, as he thought the vocal style of the music was just shrieking. Further to this, Nicolas had also been reading about the French serial killer called Remy Roy, who had lured his victims through personal advertisements: once he had met them, Roy would bludgeon them to death with a hammer. Unlike killers such as Jeffrey Dahmer, Roy did not seek companionship, nor was there any sexual element to his murders; he just wanted to watch a person die.

All the while that Nicolas was listening to music by Black Metal musicians and reading media releases regarding serial killers, he was becoming more and more consumed by his own fascination with death. All he could think about was the potential to remove the head from the corpse within the mausoleum. While everyone was talking about death, Nicolas was feeding his life through the process of death. Whether it was consuming milkshakes containing the ashes of cremations or drinking the blood of his partner in New York, Nicolas knew that he needed to surround himself with death in order to sustain the energy for his own desires. And this was only the beginning.

SIX

EVOLUTION INTO ADULT LIFE

THE PROCESS OF compartmentalisation is where a person divides different parts of their time or thoughts into a secret, metaphorical 'box'. It is a means by which a person may keep certain aspects of their personality or mindset secret from the general public, and almost, in a way, disassociate these feelings from the everyday reality that they are faced with: not necessarily putting them to the back of the mind to be forgotten about, but certainly putting the visual indicators that people may recognise out of the minds of the very individuals from whom the person wishes to keep them secret.

Not all compartmentalisation is seen as negative, however. Given that a person may have fantasies that require compartmentalisation, it could become dangerous, not only for this person but also for others around them, for these fantasies to evolve beyond mere fantasy, and actually cross into the realms of their normal, day-to-day life. This fantasy could of course be quite minor or trivial; however, sometimes it may become something else entirely...

In France, it is mandatory for all young men, when they reach a certain age, to take part in military service. Naturally, there are people who do not wish to engage in this activity, and alternative options are readily available in these situations. For example, in 1972 Nicolas' father was sent to one of the French colonies in Africa, in order to teach local people in schools. This was a typical alternative to military service for French nationals. (Of course, following this his father also worked in Africa for the banks, which is the reason that Nicolas was born in Cameroon, as the family had relocated there for a period of time.)

Nicolas at 19

In September 1992, the time had come for Nicolas to take his scheduled National Service. The mandatory period of time to be served was 10 months. Because Nicolas had been expelled from university after being found with a canister of tear gas in class and had not told his father of his expulsion, he had been roaming the grounds of Paris's cemeteries in order to fill his days. Spending time in cemeteries was not unpleasant to Nicolas by any means, as he relished the fact that he was able to fill his mornings and afternoons with something he enjoyed. However, for Nicolas to be able to do what he really loved to do, which was break into mausoleums and obtain access to coffins, mornings and afternoons were not really the best time of day.

Coupled with the fact that, as stated previously, the Père Lachaise cemetery had become the meeting spot for many of Paris's gay men, this had made certain aspects of Nicolas' wandering through cemeteries less joyful, as he now had to be alert about being approached. This alertness, as stated previously, gave Nicolas a reason to arm himself with a hammer, in order to ward off any approaches aimed in his direction. On one afternoon in the Père Lachaise cemetery, Nicolas was approached by a man, who he could feel was getting closer and closer to him, without invitation to do so. Nicolas clutched the hammer, and swung it in the direction of the man, connecting the end of the hammer with the man's head. The man fell to the ground from the impact of the hammer. The impact was not enough to kill the man; however, the impact was strong enough to have caused a serious injury such as a fracture, or a concussion. The sound of the man falling was loud enough that anyone who was close enough could hear. Therefore, Nicolas left the cemetery without further checking on the state of the fallen man.

There was no intention to kill the man, nor was this act of bludgeoning the man in any way connected to homophobic violence. The attack was simply born from Nicolas' wish to not have his personal space impeded by anyone, homosexual or not. Therefore, unlike the time when Nicolas had repeatedly stabbed the corpse of the body he had gained access to in the Russian crypt, Nicolas had no emotional attachment to hitting the man with the hammer. It was simply a form of defensive attack to ward off an uninvited approach. However, regardless of the intent of the attack, or potential resulting consequences to the fallen man, Nicolas deemed it best to not go back to the Père Lachaise cemetery for a while.

Therefore, this visit would be the last one to this cemetery for the summer – a summer when he would be leaving for military service anyway.

The thought of joining the military was not an unpleasant prospect as far as Nicolas was concerned, primarily because Nicolas knew that he would have access to guns. Considering that he had been fantasising about shooting fellow college students with a rifle from the top of the tower at the university campus, the idea of gaining access to actual weapons was a promising prospect. That summer, Nicolas had been making use of his crossbow at the Montparnasse cemetery, practising his aim by shooting at birds that were in the cemetery, a hobby that seemed to give him a great deal of joy. However, one afternoon, while Nicolas was practising his aim, a person had seen him with the crossbow. Therefore, as the person was almost out of sight, Nicolas shot a crossbow bolt in the person's direction, after which he heard the person scream. Assuming that the bolt had in fact hit the person in question, Nicolas did not hang around to find out the extent of the damage that he may have caused, as this would have almost certainly have brought with it repercussions from authorities, given the illegal nature of his hobby. At least in the military, he would at least have the possibility of using real firearms, without the risk of such potential consequences.

After having completed the required tests for his National Service, Nicolas was sent to the town of Haguenau, near Strasbourg. This was close to the German border, and to travel there, Nicolas was required to get a train from Paris to Strasbourg and then board a bus from Strasbourg to the military camp.

At the camp, Nicolas learned all about guns, he learned not only how to use guns, but also how to dismantle them and clean their parts. The main gun used by the military was the French 'Famas' rifle. This is a bullpup-style rifle, 5.56mm calibre, which was also utilised by the French Foreign Legion at the time. While capable of being fired in single-shot mode, the rifle also has a fully automatic setting which is capable of firing 900 to 1000 rounds of ammunition per minute. So quite an effective and potent rifle, in truth. When being trained how to use this, Nicolas would be on the firing range, learning how to correctly breathe while firing, as well as learning to shoot from ranges up to 200m and in addition, from a lying-down position. Once he had mastered the Famas rifle, he would also learn the art of pistol shooting on the range. Further to the actual shooting of the weapons, Nicolas would learn about the types of ammunition that could be utilised, such as 'smart' bullets, which were designed to ricochet inside the body, therefore causing as much internal damage as possible to the enemy.

Situated next to the armoury of the military base was a nuclear weapons site. This housed nuclear launchers which had the capacity to fire long-range missiles, as far as Poland, for example. The nuclear site held weapons such as Pluto missiles, which were armed with nuclear warheads. Nicolas would have loved to have been stationed for service on this site; however, it was reserved for the professional soldiers only. Therefore, any persons doing their National Service were not permitted to serve on the site. Despite Nicolas' 'hidden agenda' to access the nuclear site, in reality, this would not be possible.

Nicolas therefore worked in the basic armoury of the military camp, where his tasks included the checking of IDs when a soldier requested use of a weapon, cleaning of the guns and general paperwork duties. In addition to the Famas rifle, Nicolas was also given access to heavy-calibre (12.7mm) machine guns, which he was given the opportunity to fire once a week. On the site were armoured cars, which were used in deployment whenever required by the French Army. These carried the LRAC Bazooka. While Nicolas detested cars, he had a love of guns; he even enjoyed the menial task of cleaning the weapons.

Other than having access to weapons, Nicolas found military life tough. Most of the other soldiers were vastly different from Nicolas in both personality and background. A number of them came from housing projects and had grown up together. Owing to this, as well as the fact that very few of the soldiers shared any common cultural interests with Nicolas, such as music or even horror movies, he once again found himself feeling isolated in this social setting. The one thing that Nicolas did have on his side was that he seemed to command a deal of respect from the other soldiers. In part, this was due to the fact that Nicolas had continued to work out a lot, and therefore was more powerfully built than many of the other soldiers. This is something that Nicolas came to understand to be a common trait in varied social circles, whether it be in the military, prison, or even just in normal life: people seem to respect people who are physically stronger than they are.

During his time on the base, Nicolas did make one friend: a 19-year-old plumber, who was serving his military service at the same time. The plumber was the opposite of Nicolas in terms of personality; however, they did hang out as friends. The plumber was interested in heavy metal music, and with this as a common denominator, he would take Nicolas to local bars, where they would meet local girls. One of the reasons that the plumber seemed keen to have Nicolas as a friend was that, owing to his physique, Nicolas would attract the attention of local girls, to which by proxy would give the plumber greater access to girls – more than he would have had under normal circumstances.

At the weekends, Nicolas would be given leave from the military base, and as such, he would return to Paris on his days off. During these weekend visits home, Nicolas would hang out with his Parisian Metal friends, and in addition, he would return to frequenting cemeteries. Nicolas' collecting of macabre objects obtained from cemeteries also continued; he would gather up these items to store in his private basement. Although Nicolas would visit his friends on occasion, he was left for long periods of time in solitude.

Not one to waste his spare time, Nicolas used this time alone to contemplate what he would do once he had left the military. As he had been expelled from University, the possibility of further study seemed to not be an option, and therefore serious consideration as to a profession had to be given.

Upon watching various TV shows and seeing guests on these shows talking about their lives, Nicolas had the idea that he would like to work within the 'death industry'. The avenues of choice included the possibility of working as a pallbearer, a grave sculptor or even an embalmer. Upon further thought, it was the last of these that Nicolas decided that he would like to pursue as his career of choice. However, owing to the fact that there was still no internet to speak of at the time, he had very little access to reputable information.

The only information that Nicolas was able to obtain regarding embalming was to a school in the north of Paris which specified in embalming. The head of the school was a man called Christian Raffault, who was famous not only in embalming circles, but also in the 'death industry' as a whole. Raffault had over 30 years' experience in the field and was held in the highest regard amongst other embalming professionals.

Nicolas called the school and spoke to Christian Raffault directly. He was told what would be expected of Raffault's candidates in the school. Because Nicolas understood psychology, Nicolas was able to give Raffault reasons as to why he wished to become an embalmer. He talked about his own grandfather's funeral and said that he would like to take precise care of dead people, as a means to assist the grieving process for the family of the deceased person. Naturally, not a word of this was true, as Nicolas had his own reasons for wishing to surround himself with the dead. However, he was able to present what seemed like valid reasons as to why he would like to become an embalmer.

Not only did Raffault like Nicolas' motivation, but the young man's analysis of why he would like to join the school seemed to have struck a chord with the prestigious head of the school. Raffault went on to ask Nicolas to send in his application form, complete with a copy of his driver's licence. Contrary to belief, an embalmer was not, at this time in France, based at one particular funeral home but would instead have to travel from one funeral home to another, and to various morgues and hospitals, complete with all of the tools required for the job. Therefore a car and driving licence was an absolute necessity.

Nicolas knew then and there that his ambition of becoming an embalmer was not going to be achievable. As stated previously, Nicolas detested the thought of driving a car; therefore, even as he spoke to Raffault on the phone, he understood that even sending in an application to the school was going to be pointless. Nicolas was despondent at this unfortunate revelation. It was not as though Nicolas was unwilling to put aside his contempt for driving in order to obtain his goals. The truth is that while serving in the military, he had attempted to learn how to drive; however, this had not gone well for Nicolas.

With this in mind, Nicolas was forced to have to think about what other options that he had available, seeing as the role of an embalmer was not going to be possible. Back at the military camp, while Nicolas was pondering his next move, he was called to the office of the base's captain. This was not something that bothered Nicolas, as he was used to being called to the authorities' offices at both school and university. Nicolas wondered what the reason was for being summoned. He had been keeping autopsy magazines in his locker, so that he could read them at night, and understood that some of the other soldiers had seemed freaked out about this. Nicolas therefore thought that the magazines were going to be the subject of his conversation with the captain.

After Nicolas entered the office of the Captain, he had sat down and the Captain had begun a speech in where he said: 'My duties on the base are not only that of being your Captain, but while you are here it is also my role to be like a father figure for anything that you may need. It is with sadness that I have to tell you that your grandfather has died.'

Nicolas had mixed emotions regarding this news. On one hand, he was sad because he had actually liked his grandfather on his father's side, but from another point of view, he was quite happy and relieved at the fact that he was not being brought to the office to discuss the autopsy magazines.

Nicolas travelled back to Paris for a few days on compassionate leave. His father was naturally grieving and was therefore drinking even more than normal. Nicolas and his father were asked to go to the morgue in order to visit the body of his grandfather. The morgue was located in the posh west part of Paris, in the same region that Nicolas had discovered the open grave of the elderly Chinese woman.

Nicolas and his father entered the morgue. This was the first time that he had been inside a hospital morgue. When Nicolas went in, he seemed to have his eyes wide open. He was observing everything within the morgue, in an attempt to take in as much as he could within the short period of time that he was going to be spending there.

Nicolas was intrigued: the lights within the morgue were bright and white, giving off a very strong light. Nicolas was more concerned with paying attention to his surroundings than to his grandfather's corpse. He was taking in the *aura* of the building. Nicolas noticed that the energy that he was feeling from the building was exactly the same as the energy that he had felt in 1982, when he entered the funeral home in Brittany for his other grandfather's funeral.

In addition to the strong white lights of the morgue, the room itself was very clinical. There were three nurses in attendance, one of whom smiled at Nicolas, perhaps in sympathy towards him because of the death of his grandfather. However, Nicolas recalls not paying attention to the smile of the nurse, as he was more focused on looking at all three nurses' backsides. Then another man entered into the morgue: the morgue technician. Wearing white scrubs, he was unshaven and seemed to be very masculine in nature, with what appeared to be an animalistic aura surrounding him. The three nurses seemed to be very drawn towards the morgue technician who had entered the room. He had what Nicolas later described as a strong sexual energy about him, and therefore, instead of paying attention to the proceedings pertaining to his grandfather's body, Nicolas was instead imagining sexual scenes between the morgue technician and the three nurses in attendance.

It was at that point that Nicolas seemed to have an epiphany: he understood what it was that he wanted to do with his career. Since the possibility of becoming an embalmer was out of the question, he found solace in the fact that he could try to become a morgue technician. This was a turning point in Nicolas' life. The morgue fascinated him: by becoming a morgue technician, he would be able to indulge his morbid curiosities, as well as plunging himself into his dream of becoming a death worker.

Following the visit to the morgue, the funeral of his grandfather was due to commence. This was going to be held at the Père Lachaise cemetery. Although Nicolas knew the cemetery well, this would be the first time that he would have been able to gain access to the ovens used for cremation purposes. There was a window where he was able to peer through and actually see the coffin being placed into the oven, before a door came down and the final stage of the cremation took place. Following the completion of the cremation, he was led to the hall where the urns were kept for memorial purposes. Nicolas of course knew this section of the cemetery well: it was the very same place where he had previously obtained cremation urns not only for his basement altar, but also for the ashes themselves which he had included in his protein milkshakes. Nicolas was handed the fresh urn. Unlike all of the other urns which Nicolas had obtained in the past, this urn was still warm, a revelation that took Nicolas by surprise. He was led to the final resting place where his grandfather's urn would be kept. Once again, as Nicolas was walking through the corridor, he was reminded of the film *Phantasm*, the trailer of which he had seen while on his skiing vacation in Switzerland. This recollection, combined with where he was now in his life, gave Nicolas the sense that the circle of his activities had been completed.

After the funeral of his grandfather was complete, he returned to the military base in Strasbourg in order to resume his National Service. It was here that Nicolas devised a plan. He wanted to obtain weapons for himself. Therefore, he decided to steal weapons from the base. Nicolas was quickly able to obtain a Famas rifle and two handguns. At the time a man had been presenting a fake ID in order to obtain military weapons from barracks in the east of France. As a result, during a time in where Nicolas was alone in the armoury, he stole the Famas rifle, as well as the two .45-calibre handguns, and then blamed it on the thief who was using the fake ID. Naturally, he did not bring the weapons back to the armoury. Nicolas understood that the stealing of weapons was classed as a felony, and if caught, he would be facing imprisonment for his crimes. Not only were these weapons, but they were in fact weapons intended for war. If he were caught, he would at the very least be facing between one and two years in a military prison.

Nicolas hid the weapons in the woods until he knew that it would be safe to retrieve them. The procedure for a soldier obtaining weapons from the armoury was that the person letting them out was required to summon a superior officer for confirmation. As Nicolas did not do this, he was sent to the 'hole' for two weeks. The superior officers had suspected that Nicolas was not telling the truth; however, since not only did Nicolas play dumb about what had happened, but the superiors would also be facing charges pertaining to negligence themselves, Nicolas in a manner of speaking got away with his theft of the weapons. The guns were merely reported missing, without any further blame attached to either party.

Due to the suspicion surrounding Nicolas and the theft of the weapons, and to the fact that he was not able to be convicted for his crime – because further consequences would arise as a result of any potential conviction – Nicolas became something of a local legend amongst the soldiers based at the camp. Though, reputation aside, Nicolas understood that his plan was only half-complete at this point: he had the guns, but he still required ammunition for them. Still, in his mind, it was still halfway towards victory in terms of his plans.

As the attention surrounding the theft of the weapons began to quieten down. Nicolas understood that in order to hold onto his newly acquired weapons, he would have to compartmentalise his thoughts and keep secret his desired uses for the stolen guns. At this time, Nicolas temporarily pursued other interests, and one month later decided to go and get his very first tattoo. He got the depiction of the deity Baphomet on his arm. At the time, tattoos were not as common as they are today; therefore, the ideology not only of getting a tattoo, but of getting one of an occult deity, served to enhance his reputation within the camp. Nicolas had come to understand that such a boost in reputation, combined with the essential politics of certain social scenarios – for example, the army or prison – seems to give an individual a boost in terms of a psychological edge, as the underlying mechanics of social boosting are the same across many spectra of social interaction. As a result of this boost in standing, as it were, Nicolas became more popular amongst the other soldiers, and he came to understand that he could manipulate the other people in awe of him to do whatever he wanted them to, or even to just get his own way. This would prove to be a valuable life lesson for Nicolas for the future.

Nicolas at 20

In October 1993, Nicolas had completed his National Military Service and was now focused on obtaining a job within a morgue. He drew up a list of hospitals that he understood to have morgues located within them. The list comprised almost 50 hospitals in total, and as a result, Nicolas sent out 50 CVs, one to each of the hospitals. The following week, Nicolas received a phone call from a hospital in the 14th District of Paris, the famous St Vincent du Paul: a hospital known for paediatrics and made famous in medieval times for being a place where mothers would lay their unwanted children at the gates or doors of the hospital, which would take the children in and care for them.

Nicolas was called for an interview at this famous hospital. He was nervous for the interview, particularly so because he knew that he really wanted to get the job, and he knew that he would have to prepare in advance. He would be able to present himself well for the interview, without giving away any indication of his motives, and not appear insane.

When he arrived at the hospital for the interview, Nicolas was presented to a woman in the human resources department, who appeared to be in her fifties. During the interview Nicolas spoke of his military service, his one year of psychological studies, and said that he wished to assist families during the entire grieving process. Again, this was not the truth, but Nicolas understood that this was a better alternative to telling her that he had been expelled from university for having a tear gas canister in his bag, and that he had four years of grave-robbing experience to his name! The interview went well, and he was told that he could start a two-week trial on the following Monday. His role was essentially to replace a person who was going to be on two weeks' vacation.

That Monday, Nicolas arrived at the hospital and was informed what his duties would be. He was to be an assistant to the morgue technician in the mornings, and then he would assist in the radiology department in the afternoons. Nicolas had no interest in the radiology department; however, as he was being allowed to work within the morgue in the morning, sacrificing his afternoons in radiology was a small price to pay in order to achieve his ultimate goals.

Nicolas was shown around the morgue and in turn was introduced to the morgue technician. The man was an ex-paratrooper, and Nicolas sensed immediately that he was a weird person. The man bragged of the war zones that he had been in, even as he acted normally while the woman from HR was there. However, as soon as the woman left the morgue, Nicolas understood that the man was in fact, completely insane. The technician showed Nicolas to a room where he kept a punching bag, which naturally Nicolas found strange. As it turns out, the man was constantly on edge, and was constantly yelling at people for no apparent reason. On one occasion, Nicolas recalls the morgue technician losing his temper while on duty, and instead of going into the other room to punch his punching bag, he instead took out his frustrations on a corpse within the morgue, and as result began punching the deceased body. To Nicolas' surprise, though, and despite the man constantly yelling at everyone else, he seemed to like Nicolas.

In the morgue itself, which was located on the underground levels of the hospital, there were two main rooms, one of which was the autopsy room, and the other was the family waiting room, which basically comprised a couch. The insane morgue technician bragged to Nicolas of having sex with nurses on the couch, which Nicolas thought was nothing more than lies. Later, however, Nicolas, seeing the man bring nurses to the room when there was no work being undertaken, understood that this crazy revelation was in fact true.

Another revelation that Nicolas was to uncover was that, in many sections of the morgue, there were a large number of dusty glass jars, kept in what seemed to be every cupboard inside the morgue, as well as under all manner of tables – in fact, in every possible storage area that there was within the morgue. Inside these glass jars were the remains of recently aborted foetuses, which had been extracted and placed into these jars in order to be preserved, which gave the impression that this was the life's collection of some crazy abortionist. The foetuses were not, however, placed in the jars carefully. Some were shoved crudely into the jars, and others even had their heads detached from the aborted bodies and were just floating at the top of the sealed jars. There were hundreds of them in total. Nicolas didn't question why the foetuses were being kept in the jars: he presumed that they were being held for some form of medical museum. Therefore, he had no inclination that they were in fact the collections of a deranged doctor.

In the morgue, behind a large metallic door, was a cold chamber which turned out to be the fridges where bodies were stored for autopsy. As the hospital was primarily a children's hospital, several bodies of young children were stored in the fridges. In the corner of the room was a table, in where the body of a young black girl, seven or eight years old at her time of death, who was being readied for autopsy. The morgue technician was essentially going to be testing Nicolas to see if he was going to be able to withstand the job. This would be the very first autopsy that Nicolas would be taking part in; not only that, but this was on his first day. Nicolas understood that the morgue technician had done this on purpose in order to see if Nicolas was suitable for the job. What the technician did not understand, though, was that while Nicolas felt a degree of sadness at the fact that it was a young girl that was deceased, as a whole Nicolas was impressed by the entire situation and scenario. Therefore, there was no hesitation from Nicolas when he was told to prepare himself by wearing all of the required protective equipment and clothing.

Autopsies of children are a very common procedure: naturally, it is not usual that a child should die at such a young age, so it is often considered necessary to perform autopsies on children to determine the reason for their premature death. Autopsies are generally performed by a doctor; a morgue technician is there to assist him, usually by weighing the organs and also passing the required instruments to the doctor. Prior to these procedures, a morgue technician is required to learn the names of all of the instruments that are used. During the autopsy, Nicolas was able to observe how the Y-shaped incision was made in the upper torso of the deceased, and also saw how the body was opened up so that all of the organs were revealed. The doctor would then remove the organs and place them into small boxes so that they could be weighed. In observing this, Nicolas was essentially given an anatomy lesson.

The doctor who performed the autopsy was very condescending towards Nicolas, primarily because of his youth. His comments towards Nicolas were somewhat snide, and as a result, Nicolas did not like him. At times, the incisions into the body would be done by the morgue technician, should the doctor be busy. Nicolas would learn how to make the main incision on the head, where the skin on the head could be peeled back to reveal the skull. Then a circular buzz saw designed specifically to saw through the bone was used, so that the person performing the autopsy would be able to access the brain. Nicolas found these different instruments extremely fascinating. He understood immediately that this was the job that he wished to do; there was not a single question in his mind regarding this. As stated, Nicolas did find it sad that it was a little girl that the autopsy was being carried out on; however, his fascination for the job at hand overshadowed any feelings of potential sadness. Therefore Nicolas was emotionally detached towards the autopsy, as his interests lay in focussing on what was happening.

After the doctor had left, Nicolas and the morgue technician took the boxes containing the organs to the lab to be tested. Following this, they went back to the deceased girl on the autopsy table and Nicolas was shown how to fill the voids in the body where the organs had been taken from, as well as how to stitch the incisions up. To Nicolas' surprise, the morgue technician pulled out a large bunch of newspapers. He then scrunched the newspapers into balls and began to stuff the empty torso cavities and cranium cavities with these balls of newspapers. Ideally, a special kind of cotton balls are used to fill with cavities within the various sections of the body, but as it turns out, newspaper does the job just as well, and is a fraction of the cost in comparison.

Following this, Nicolas was shown how to do what is called 'restoration stitching', which ensures that the corpse does not leak any additional fluids after the autopsy. The mouth of the deceased is then sewn shut, as a means to preserve the body. This is done by placing the needle inside one nostril and through the septum; the mouth is then stitched from the inside out, therefore preserving a more natural look. However, prior to stitching the mouth close, cotton balls are placed down the throat of the deceased, as a means to further prevent leakage.

Once the body of the young girl was filled with newspaper and stitched closed, the body was cleaned with a sponge and a hose. Following this, the girl was then placed into her communion dress. This is difficult in itself, as the dress needed to be put on the body without having to cut the material. Nicolas found that putting the white communion gloves onto the girl's hands were in fact the most difficult task, as her fingers had begun to become twisted with rigor mortis. A small tiara was then placed on the young girl's head. There was no embalming done to the corpse, as the body still had fluid blood in the system. Therefore, following the re-dressing of the young girl, their work was complete.

This was Nicolas' first autopsy. He certainly felt a mix of emotions with regards to this. There was the immediate attraction to the job, and to the entire procedure that had ensued, and a certain degree of natural fascination with being a death worker, just as there had been a natural fascination with death for the majority of his life to that point. When Nicolas went home that day, he had trouble sleeping, as the mix of various emotions continued to swirl inside his mind: the fascination, the excitement of being in that environment. Despite the constant flow of varied emotions, Nicolas was looking forward to his next day at the morgue.

As Nicolas' contract was for a two-week period, he was called into HR to undergo a series of questions and tests in order to see what his compatibility would be in terms of being offered a permanent contract. As part of the tests, Nicolas was required to see a psychiatrist as a mandatory section of the testing process. Despite his parents having been told in the past by school teachers and headmasters that psychiatric evaluation would be of benefit to Nicolas, this was in fact his first ever interaction with a mental health professional. Some of the tests were also of a cognitive nature, in order to assess Nicolas' overall suitability for the role. Nicolas was asked if there were any aspects of the job that he found difficult, to which the natural answer was of course that there were not. As with Nicolas' initial interview with the woman from the HR department, Nicolas again told lies about wanting to assist in the grieving process for the families. In addition, Nicolas stated that not only was he not negatively influenced by his role within the morgue, but also that he was motivated to learn more.

Despite having performed well, in his view, on these evaluations, the HR department informed him that there had been another person who had answered the series of questions in a more suitable manner, and that an older and more experienced person was preferred for the role. Nicolas did not entirely believe that to be the whole truth, and as a result, suspected that there must have been something in his evaluation that the psychiatrist had been alerted to.

On the final day of his short contract, Nicolas was left in the morgue on his own. At the end of the day, he was to return to HR to drop in his keys and hospital badge and pick up his final pay cheque. However, before he did any of this, Nicolas went to the cupboard where many of the glass jars containing aborted foetuses were kept. He decided to remove two of the jars from the cupboard, wrap them in towels, and place them into his bag, so that he could take them home with him before he left the hospital for the final time. He then rearranged the jars in the cupboard so that no one would notice the missing jars for several months, by which time Nicolas would have been long gone from the hospital and subsequently would not be suspected of taking the glass jars. He left his bag at the door to HR, dropped off the items that he was required to, and upon saying his goodbyes, picked up his bag, with the foetus jars inside, and made his way home from the hospital.

Coincidentally, some 11 years later, a woman who wished to know what had become of her aborted foetus made enquiries to the hospital, at which point the hospital then discovered the hundred or so glass jars (minus two, of course) which contained the aborted foetuses. These were, in actual fact, supposed to have been cremated and disposed of. When the hospital discovered that these jars existed, they assumed that the doctor had held the aborted remains in order to do research. As it turns out, however, no research was ever done; in fact, the doctor had kept the foetuses for his own purposes. This turned out to be a huge scandal in the French media, and when all of the jars were located, it turned out to be vastly more than a hundred preserved foetuses, the total number of jars actually being 353. The scandal was dubbed 'The Meathouse of Lost Children' by the press, and following an investigation, many people, including the doctor who had collected them, were fired from their hospital positions. When Nicolas saw this in the news, he realised that he could have in fact stolen even more jars and got away with it.

In the aftermath of leaving the morgue, Nicolas began to think that the morgue technician played a part in him not being offered a permanent position. This may have been due to the fact that Nicolas himself was gaining positive attention from the nurses within the hospital, so that the morgue technician perhaps purposely sabotaged his application out of sheer jealousy. Nevertheless, by compartmentalising his thoughts and motives with regard to obtaining a morgue position, he was free to continue his search for another position within another morgue. The fact that he had not been fired or let go under dubious circumstances laid the path the continue in his search of death work, without ever giving insight as to his true intentions.

SEVEN

FANTASY BROUGHT TO LIFE

Mere Thoughts Becoming
A Physical Entity

THERE IS A point in every convicted killer's timeline – as well as those who have not yet been convicted or even apprehended – where the thoughts and fantasises in their minds cross the border from the realms of idealistic thought into some form of physical reality: for example, with Ted Bundy, where the fantasies of killing and abusing a young woman became something more than just a thought in his mind and actually came to fruition.

Now it would be absurd to suggest that Bundy or those like him go from one day fantasising about killing to the next day actually carrying out their heinous deeds; there must be a progression of events, or even, if you like, a subsequent devolution. Of course, the ultimate motive behind Bundy's deeds were murder and the abuse and mutilation of his victim's corpse that followed, but he simply did not fantasise about it one day and proceed to murder the next. It started with what you could liken to dipping his toes in the water. For Bundy, it has been recorded that he began his physical exploits by becoming a 'peeping Tom'. From there, each criminal thing that Bundy did was done as a series of stepping stones towards what he would eventually devolve into. Each one of his devolution steps would have been classed in his mind as breaking some form of a barrier, whether criminal, emotional or even mental: each would need to have been overcome before the taboos of killing and abuse were extinguished in their entirety.

We must remember, too, that such 'barriers' are not purely the province of people such as Ted Bundy, or even criminals as a whole. All of us do this, in a manner of speaking. As adolescents, we do not just delve into drinking, getting drunk and developing a taste for alcohol as a whole. In truth, most of us, when we have our first taste of alcohol, recoil a little at the harsh aftertaste, yet we drink a little more until the barriers that are held within our taste buds are vanquished, and then we are able to enjoy an alcoholic drink without so much as a second thought about that initial taste.

The criminal process is no different. At first, the person deemed a criminal may not even be dabbling in what would be considered criminal acts; however, what we don't realise is that each 'dabble' is the stepping stone to what could potentially become the ultimate act, and before others become aware of this, the pathway has been navigated so far that the natural progression is to move forward and bring the fantasies to fruition, regardless of the ultimate goal.

Following Nicolas' departure from working in the morgue at St Vincent de Paul, there were two essential additions to his life. The first was that Nicolas now had important morgue experience that he could put down on his CV, which would be invaluable for obtaining a new job at another morgue in Paris. Second was the acquisition of the jars containing aborted foetuses, which Nicolas was able to take home and place upon the altar located in his private basement, within the house that he shared with his father.

Having placed the two jars on his altar, Nicolas would offer prayers as part of his spiritual beliefs. In one of the jars, the head of the foetus had become detached from the rest of the body and was now floating at the top of the sealed jar. Nicolas decided to open the jar and see what it smelled like. However, when he did so, he could only smell the preserving fluid formaldehyde. This smell was extremely strong; in truth, it hurt his eyes when he took in the toxic fumes from the jar. The sensation was not dissimilar to the feeling one would get when encountering mace or tear gas. Like those substances, the formaldehyde caused Nicolas to cough a great deal when he inhaled the fumes. In addition, the formaldehyde acts on a human being as a carcinogen, that is, has cancer-inducing properties. As a matter of precaution, therefore, Nicolas stopped smelling the contents of the aborted foetus jars.

Instead of smelling the jars, Nicolas decided to remove the detached head from one of the jars, and placed it on a heater, as though to dry the head, or even mummify the head so that it could be turned into a decorative and spiritual necklace. However, after only two weeks, Nicolas discovered that the removed head had begun to change colour, and so he decided to put it back into the jar, placing the jar back upon his altar. In truth, Nicolas relished the fact that the altar was taking shape: it almost seemed to him as if the two jars contained two separate souls which had been ritualistically sacrificed to the altar.

Following his release from St Vincent de Paul hospital, Nicolas had continued to send out CVs to all of the other hospitals with morgues in them. In November of 1993, he received word that he was to be given an interview at St Joseph's, a hospital in the 14th District of Paris. While Nicolas was waiting for his impending interview at St Joseph's, he continued to hang out with his heavy metal friends. It was through these connections that Nicolas became acquainted with a group that was into 'Hardcore' Punk. Part of this group were essentially skinheads. It was not as though Nicolas was particularly fond of these people; however, Nicolas had an ulterior motive for his newfound friendship with the skinheads. One of the people in this group worked in a gun shop, and as Nicolas still had the three firearms that he had stolen during his time in the military, he surmised that sparking a friendship with this person was going to be the easiest route to obtaining ammunition for his guns, all the while keeping the fact that he had these weapons a secret even from the person who actually worked in the gun shop. In truth, Nicolas did not really feel as though he was able to trust these people, not only with the fact that he had the stolen weapons, but also with the fact that he had an altar with items obtained in what could be deemed a criminal manner. He felt as though the members of the skinhead group would almost certainly inform the police of these facts. Therefore, he decided to not only keep the details of the altar a secret, but also the fact that he had the guns, along with any potential motive he might have for obtaining ammunition. For a group of people who professed to be anti-establishment and supposedly into the macabre, Nicolas always felt as though they were not only fake but also talked far too much. There would almost certainly be one person among their ranks who would sing like a canary to the authorities.

While Nicolas was on the hunt for ammunition, he continued to hang out with the people from this group and do things such as going to concerts. While at one concert, he met one of his friends whose girlfriend had a friend who was also single. Therefore, it was suggested that Nicolas go on a date with this single girl, so the four of them could double-date. Nicolas would later recall that she was a nice girl who worked in a fancy fashion shop in Paris, near where he was living. As a result, he would go and visit her at work, after he was finished with what he had been doing throughout the day. Nicolas recalls doing a ritual in front of his altar, in which he swore that if he was successful in his job interview, he would sacrifice the soul of the girl to Satan in exchange. Nicolas did not know how he would make this sacrifice; in truth, he was drunk when he made this promise to the altar.

Nicolas continued to date the girl, and as the two got to know each other more, the more their flirting evolved. One day, as the girl was finishing work and the store was closing, the pair locked the front door and went to the back area of the shop, where they proceeded to have sex. However, what the girl did not know, was that Nicolas, prior to meeting up with her, had undertaken a ritual: he opened the packaging of a condom with a scalpel and, having removed the condom, proceeded to rub it onto one of the foetuses from the jars, essentially covering the condom in foetus juice. The reasoning for doing this was that by then using the condom when having sex with the girl, he would be able to inject foetus juice into her. Nicolas was fully aware that had the girl known what he was doing, she would have most certainly have left him. The truth was that Nicolas did not actually care about that possibility; however, he still decided to not tell her. Even after they had finished, Nicolas did not tell the girl. However, it did give Nicolas a strange sense of satisfaction, as if the girl had been having sex with the Grim Reaper, even if she did not have any clue that she was doing so. For his part, Nicolas felt as though his ritual had served to satisfy his part in the ritual in front of the altar. In other words, in Nicolas' mind, it was this adaptation of the ritual that had saved the girl from being murdered and her soul offered up as a sacrifice to Satan.

In short, Halloween of 1993 was a fun time for Nicolas, regardless of whether other people were aware of it or not. Following his ritualistic desecration of the condom, and after his continued prayers to deities such as Pazuzu and Belial in front of his altar, Nicolas received some good news: he had been successful in his job interview for the role of morgue attendant at St Joseph's Hospital. The person who had been conducting the interview did not ask Nicolas any strange questions where he would have tripped himself up, and as such, given away any of his real motives for wanting to work in the morgue.

The exterior of St Joseph's morgue

St Joseph's was a Catholic hospital dating from the 17th century: as such, it principally catered for patients of the Catholic faith. Therefore, unlike the overwhelming majority of morgues in other hospitals in Paris, which were for deceased people of all denominations, the morgue of St Joseph's had a Catholic chapel attached to the morgue, in which religious ceremonies connected with the person's death would take place. In addition, Catholic members of the parish would use the chapel to pray, seeking guidance and solace from the Catholic priest in attendance at the chapel.

The Priest in attendance at the chapel within St Joseph's morgue would not only perform religious ceremonies, but was also there to perform the Last Rites ceremony on the deceased. This is a ritual that all practising Catholics are entitled to when they are about to die. The Priest, Prêtre Morand, not only worked at St Joseph's hospital, but also practised as a professional exorcist for Paris' famous Notre Dame Cathedral. By this time Morand had become quite famous as an exorcist and had written several books on exorcism, as well as appearing on French Television as an expert on the subject.

Inside St Joseph's Hospital, the morgue was situated near the rear of the building, adjacent to where the refuse for the hospital would be disposed of. The morgue itself was split into two separate levels: a lower level where the fridges and trays containing the bodies were kept and the autopsies were carried out; and an upper level comprising the office for any paperwork and other administration in connection with the morgue, as well as a family room, where families would wait for their appointments. And then of course there was the Chapel, where Morand would conduct his ceremonies.

Nicolas has described Morand as being obsessed with Satanism and the Devil; he would talk to Nicolas on this subject at length. He claimed to have visions: he stated that on one occasion in the chapel he had seen the Devil there and had then cast the Devil out by means of exorcism. Apparently, the Devil had been standing in the exact same spot where Nicolas was now standing as they spoke. Nicolas found this to be amusing: not only did he get the sense that Morand was fond of him, but it also seemed to him that Morand had actually failed to expel the Devil, since he was obviously unaware as to Nicolas' exploits, not only up until that point in time, but also what was to come. Nicolas has later stated that he would have loved to have seen the look on Morand's face after the news of Nicolas' arrest broke. It was especially amusing to Nicolas that, despite Morand's seemingly extensive talents as an exorcist, he was unable to cast Nicolas out. Nicolas was, after all, a very young and intense 'Soldier of Satan', as it were.

Nicolas found it quite ironic that he had been hired to work in a morgue that was not only Christian, but highly devout, considering that his own, absolutely contradictory beliefs represented, in a sense, total blasphemy. Nicolas likened himself to a 'Devil in Disguise', much like a wolf in sheep's clothing. When Nicolas was alone and unsupervised in the chapel, he would conduct himself in a manner that would certainly have been deemed blasphemous, such as bringing girls into the chapel and engaging in sexual acts on the altar, or masturbating into the font containing holy water. Nicolas basically did all that he could to desecrate the holiness of the chapel, as a direct insult not only to the building, but to God Himself.

Nicolas has stated his utter contempt for the vast majority of latter-day 'Satanists', as these particular people seem to be more image-oriented – e.g. the wearing of symbols such as pentagrams and inverted crosses. In Nicolas' eyes, these people are nothing more than posers who are trying to invoke a degree of superficial controversy. With the exception of a small group of Norwegian Black Metal musicians, who committed murder and burned churches to the ground in the early 1990s, the vast majority of modern Satanists are active in image only; as such, Nicolas regards them as more repulsive than fundamentalist Christians: at least the Christians, despite holding completely opposite belief systems to Nicolas, act out on these beliefs and practise what they preach. The modern-day Satanist, as a rule, does not.

When Nicolas started work at the morgue, its technical team was made up of three people. There had been a fourth member of the team; however, this person had taken time off work as a result of depression and was therefore going to be off for an undetermined amount of time. This had resulted in the requirement for another person to be added to the team: in other words, Nicolas.

The leader – technically manager – of the department was a man in his mid to late 50s. He was tall and skinny and had an oddly shaped nose, which made him somewhat resemble a vulture in appearance, complete with a set of dark eyes behind the crooked nose. In Nicolas' own words, he was 'ugly as fuck'. Of the other two men who worked in the morgue, one was courting the vulture's daughter, and the other was the soon-to-be 'son-in-law's' best friend. It was almost as though the entirety of the morgue team was made up of a sort of family circle. As Nicolas was the newest member of the team and not a part of the trio's 'family circle', he was almost immediately alienated from the rest of the group. This was not dissimilar to almost every other social encounter that Nicolas had been exposed to in his life. At that point in time, the members of the circle did not trust Nicolas and kept him on the outside, as if to make him feel as though he did not belong. He was treated as though he were sent as a spy from headquarters, to oversee what was going on inside of the morgue and report back. Naturally, none of this was true; however, the trio nevertheless remained very protective of their 'family circle'.

The morgue itself was very old both in terms of architecture and equipment. The ceiling of the morgue was very high and almost gave the room a Gothic feel; a large number of the tiled walls had broken slates, while the autopsy tables themselves were made out of old marble slabs. The equipment inside was similarly old: even the trolleys on which the equipment and bodies were carted around would squeak when they were moved. Nicolas loved the look of the décor of the morgue: it was almost as though the morgue was from a 1920s horror movie – or, to use a more up-to-date reference, like something out of the TV series *American Horror Story*.

Inside the lower room, there were at least 30 fridge units in which the deceased were kept awaiting autopsy. Further down the corridor was the main autopsy room. The room was extremely large, almost 25 square metres in size: to this day, it is the largest autopsy room that Nicolas has ever seen. Upstairs from the autopsy room was the chapel, which in turn had three separate rooms where ceremonies were undertaken. As a deceased body could not be taken up the stairs, there was an old lift used for this purpose.

The lift itself, like so much else, was old and in vintage fashion. It had a squeaky but retractable gate which the user had to close before it could be operated. The lift chamber itself was incredibly small, only big enough for the trolley transporting the deceased and the morgue attendant manoeuvring it. Quite often, due to the age of its deteriorating mechanisms, the lift would become stuck between one floor and the next, which could cause a person of a timid disposition to become scared or unsettled. However, not only did Nicolas relish the prospect of being able to work within the morgue, he also loved the antiquity of the rooms and structures.

The working hours of the morgue were, for the most part, Monday to Friday, with the requirement for weekend work being one weekend out of three. The boss himself never worked the weekend, as it was his position to have to do the relevant paperwork for the morgue and patients. For that very same reason of paperwork, Nicolas found himself having to work at least two or three of the weekdays alone, as the boss was more often than not engaged in paperwork or other duties. What Nicolas later discovered was that the boss was doing private work for a funeral home as well – work that, as it turned out, was illegal in nature. In France, morgues are not in any way connected to funeral homes; as such, when a body is released to the family for burial or cremation, it is the choice of the deceased person's relatives as to which funeral home to use for burial services. What the boss was essentially doing was referring the deceased person's family to the funeral home that he was also working for; in turn, he would receive a commission as part of the funeral expense. In France, this is an offence that can actually result in a jail sentence. However, it is done regardless. The general cost of a funeral can be anything from 2000 to 10,000 Euros; as such, a few hundred Euros as a fraudulent commission for referrals was unlikely to be noticed.

Each year, funeral homes would send the morgue attendants gifts such as bottles of champagne and food parcels to bribe them into giving the funeral homes referrals for newly deceased bodies. The trio in the 'family circle' would no doubt have been apprehensive that Nicolas might perhaps tell the relevant authorities. Nicolas, however, was completely unaware that this was illegal. Even if he had have known, he would not have cared: he understood why they were doing this, as a morgue attendant's salary was not large, so making a bit of extra money from exploits such as these was not something that concerned him.

There were other activities, such as the dressing of the bodies, that were not the required responsibility of the morgue attendants. However, funeral homes would bribe the morgue attendants to perform these roles as it made their own jobs easier. Again, Nicolas was only later made aware that it was in fact illegal to take money for doing this job. Again, though, Nicolas did not care: he understood that the need for extra cash was worth the risk.

This was not all that the morgue attendants did outside the rules. As a strict rule, all autopsies were required to be done by a doctor, and morgue attendants were not allowed to make incisions of any kind on the bodies. The role of the morgue attendant was only to weigh the organs passed to them by the doctors and to hand them the tools that they required. Then, once the autopsy had been completed, the morgue attendant was required to do the stitching up of the body, to prevent leakage. However, because the attending doctors rarely wished to spend much time in the morgue performing the autopsies, they would often get an attendant to do the majority of the work – sometimes all of it. As an average, an autopsy would take between one and two hours to complete, however, with the doctor taking such a cavalier approach to the job, it seemed as though the maximum time that they would spend in the morgue would be roughly 40 minutes at the most. Although this was completely illegal, the morgue attendant would have to undertake the role of looking for abnormalities during the autopsy, when this was of course the doctor's job. However, Nicolas ignored the doctor's crooked misdirection of his role; in fact, he would use these opportunities to learn a lot about the body, and how to dissect bodies. Further to this, he also learned how to efficiently run a morgue.

During the time at the morgue, Nicolas would notice that the boss would spend large amounts of time away from the others when on duty, and would only appear when a particular nurse came to the offices. The nurse was at least 20 years younger than the boss and was quite pretty, other than the fact that she had a large nose. The nurse, of course, was the boss's mistress, but what Nicolas could not fathom was why the young nurse would have any interest in the old boss, especially as the boss was extremely repulsive to look at. Later Nicolas would discover that the boss had offered to pay for the young nurse to have cosmetic surgery on her nose in exchange for sexual favours. What the boss hadn't anticipated was the that young nurse had noticed Nicolas when she had come to the morgue department and had developed a sexual interest in him. One afternoon, when Nicolas was working in the morgue alone on his designated weekend, the nurse visited him at the morgue under the ruse that she had left her scarf in the offices. The scarf had indeed been left there; however, she had done so on purpose, so she could collect it at a time when she knew that Nicolas would be working alone. Nicolas began to see the young nurse as a means of a casual and secret sexual relationship. It was not as though Nicolas felt any form of emotional connection to her; however, he did take relish in the fact that he could use this as a form of revenge on his boss for treating him as an outsider and attempting to alienate him in the job that he had been so desperate to obtain. Naturally Nicolas did not wish to be fired from what was his ultimate dream job, so his revenge on his boss remained a secret. Still, he took comfort from the fact that while the boss obtained sexual favours from the nurse for money, Nicolas was able to obtain just as much out of nothing other than her attraction to him.

Out of the remainder of the staff that worked in the morgue, Nicolas did not get on with the man who was dating the boss's daughter, but he did get on, to a degree, with the other man, who happened to be the best friend of the boss's 'son-in-law'. Nicolas discovered that this person did not actually like the job within the morgue, and in truth would have preferred to study Technical Drawing and become something like an architect. However, he had no option other than to work in the morgue as a way of paying his bills and sustaining his day-to-day lifestyle.

Nicolas decided to try to devise a plan. Although he got on with the one person, as a whole, he could not stand the company of the three of them. He wished to attempt to get rid of them all, and following that, to work with people who would be better company and more suited to the role – and preferably be girls. As a ruse, Nicolas decided to befriend the one of the trio that he could stand a little, and following a few drinks at a local bar, went back to the man's house with him, which was only a 15-minute walk from the hospital. In his pocket Nicolas had an Opinel folding knife, which though large could be easily concealed if required. When he was at the man's house, Nicolas studied its layout, made a note of where the neighbour's entrances were, checked the areas surrounding the house. In addition, when he entered the house, he found out the man's door entry code and memorised it so that he could gain easy entry into the building.

The pair sat in the man's living room and drank whiskey while they talked. Nicolas found the man extremely boring, especially as the man's primary interest was football, which Nicolas not only had zero interest in but also detested both as a sport and as a topic of conversation. The entire time the man was talking, Nicolas began to stare at the man's throat, and it was not long until all that Nicolas could think about was taking the Opinel knife and cutting the man's throat with it. His thoughts grew from a basic fantasy to a series of chaotic thoughts. In his mind Nicolas would grab the man by the jaw, lift his head in an upwards direction and proceed to slash the man's throat with one foul thrust of the blade.

In what could only be described as a moment of clarity, the man began to talk about the work that the two shared. This was indeed a crucial injection into the conversation that evening, as Nicolas suddenly remembered that the man, although extremely boring and, in Nicolas' mind, deserving of death, was also in fact a 'death worker', as Nicolas saw it. As such, the man's line of work afforded him a modicum of respect from Nicolas.

As he sat there, Nicolas felt contradictory motives. He understood that if the man were killed and out of the picture, as it were, this would take Nicolas one step closer to his ultimate goal of ridding himself of the entire trio that worked alongside him in the morgue. However, he concluded that due to the fact that he worked with this man, it would open up the possibility that he would be a suspect if there were an investigation into the man's death – not to mention the small amount of respect that he held towards the man, purely out of the sense that they shared a bond as fellow 'death workers'. Therefore, Nicolas decided to leave the knife in his pocket and not use it on his colleague, while still maintaining a personal sense of pride and satisfaction that he held the power of both life and death of this man in his hands at this point in time. In Nicolas' mind, this was not dissimilar to the power that Caesar would have had over the lives of the gladiators in the Colosseum in times of ancient Rome.

The man was indeed extremely lucky: until this point, Nicolas had intended to end the man's life in his own residence. When Nicolas had previously bludgeoned the gay man with a hammer in the cemetery, there had been no emotional attachment to the attack; Nicolas considered it self-defence. This time, however, he felt an emotional attachment to the scenario: despite not carrying out his planned attack, there was the sense of empowerment that Nicolas felt he held over his colleague, as he had fully intended to carry out his wishes and desires. The motive for killing the man would have been more out of a sense of gratification and fun than for self-defence.

Following the decision to let his work colleague live, Nicolas resumed his duties at the morgue. Nicolas was to assist a doctor with an adult autopsy. He had already learned all the technical terms for the equipment, as well as the specific purpose of each. Further to this, Nicolas was already quite skilled at stitching up the deceased body once the autopsy had been completed. On this occasion, the autopsy was to be conducted on the body of a recently deceased Catholic priest. As the priest had died of a suspected brain tumour, the doctor would need to extract the brain in order to confirm the diagnosis. Nicolas was prepared for the forthcoming autopsy and was dressed in the required protective clothing. The doctor then appeared, wearing no protective equipment whatsoever, not even autopsy boots – footwear specifically designed for the process of an autopsy, which would normally be considered necessary, as a lot of waste material usually finds its way onto the floor during the procedure. Not only was the doctor not wearing any of the required protective clothing, he was dressed quite formally, in a suit and tie: a ridiculous outfit in the circumstances.

The doctor cut around the skull with a scalpel, then began cutting the bone of the skull with a saw. When the top of the skull was removed, the brain, which is usually a solid material even after death, seemed to be nearly liquid in consistency. The solid matter inside the skull, which was the remnants of the brain, slid out of the open skull and onto the floor, splattering the doctor's nice, expensive shoes. When the surprised doctor exclaimed, 'Oh fuck!', Nicolas found it nigh-on impossible to hold in his laughter at the man's negligence. This situation was not helped by the fact that as the doctor walked away from the autopsy table, he was having to tread on the leftover brain matter in shoes already saturated with 'brain juice', a scenario which Nicolas found highly amusing.

Once the brain had been removed and the remainder of the autopsy was carried out, Nicolas noticed that the inner parts of the deceased priest's body seemed completely different from what he had seen before. For example, when Nicolas had assisted with the young black girl's autopsy at the St Vincent de Paul's mortuary, he had noticed that the inner organs of the young girl seemed to be very neat and relatively well kept, considering that she was deceased. In stark contrast to the young girl, however, the priest was very overweight, and when his body was opened up, the entire network of organs seemed to be covered in what Nicolas would later describe as a yellow 'cobweb'. This cobweb was in fact layers of fat that had encompassed the entirety of the priest's organs. Further to this, the inside of the priest's body emitted an extremely foul-smelling odour. Although the priest had neglected to look after his health while he was still alive, the remainder of the autopsy was carried out with great care. Clearly, the doctor clearly did not wish to be covered in any more vile fluids from the priest's body, but Nicolas also noted that even though the patient would obviously not feel a thing, the incisions were done in a soft and delicate manner. As a result, according to Nicolas, no more 'liquid shit' burst from the cavities.

Once the required examinations of the autopsy were complete, the doctor showed Nicolas how to drill the bones when closing the corpse up. Nicolas would later describe the drilling of the bone as similar to that of going to the dentist and getting a cavity after a tooth was removed. The doctor then showed Nicolas how to stitch up the body, not knowing that Nicolas already knew how to do this. However, Nicolas listened to the doctor anyway: he figured he would be able to adapt these teachings to improve his own skill set with regards to stitching up a corpse.

Once everything with regards to the autopsy was complete, it was mandatory for all participants to take a shower, for the obvious reason that deceased bodies carry with them a number of toxins that develop during the various degrees of decomposition. Once he had completed his shower, Nicolas was surprised to see the doctor washing his socks in a basin and then placing them onto a heater to dry quickly, so that he could wear them again after the autopsy. Nicolas found this to be extremely miserly, especially considering that the price of a new pair of socks was not that expensive. This is something that Nicolas would discover time and time again: not only were the majority of the doctors that he encountered quite stingy about spending money, but they also seemed to be no more than a crowd of ageing alcoholics. Further, the doctors who performed forensic medicine appeared to be amongst the worst of them. This was a trend that served to give doctors the uncomplimentary title of 'alcoholics with diplomas'. It just goes to show that even those with the most revered public positions have traits below the surface that can make people see them in a completely different light.

EIGHT

DIFFERENT SPHERES OF REALITY

Crossing a Boundary from where There Is No Return

WHEN YOU DELVE deeper into the mind of a criminal, especially one considered to have a psychotic nature, there are, of course, different categories and even sub-categories beyond that. While it is very easy to label all serial killers and murders as psychopaths, it would be very naive to do so.

The truth is that the majority of convicted murderers can be divided into two main categories: the psychopath and the sociopath. Studies will say that the main difference between the two is that while psychopaths show zero signs of remorse, sociopaths will at least show a small degree of remorse and emotion with regards to the crimes that they have committed.

Having spoken to convicted murderers, I feel that these categories only scratch the surface of what goes on within the criminal mind. One point, often overlooked, is that not only will a psychopath show no remorse, they will also give very little regard to the consequences of their crimes. Therefore, the psychopath could be said to act out primarily on 'animal instinct' alone, taking the approach that they will do what they want to do when they want to do it and not caring about what might happen afterwards, much in the same manner that a spoilt child will throw a tantrum when they are told 'no' and cannot get what they want. For example, a rapist does not take the clear indications of non-consent from their victim as a signal to stop them from getting what they want. Much in the same way a tantrum-throwing child will not consider the consequences of their actions, the rapist does not think about what may come after, and at the time is entirely focused on sexual gratification.

Then we observe the mindset of a sociopath. A person in this category may well plot their crime in detail, perhaps constructing a series of deceptions, and when they find difficulties in obtaining what they want, they may seek alternative means for whatever their gratification would be, while still keeping their mind focused on their ultimate goal. The main reason for this is they are able to understand the concept of being told no, even though they know that this detracts from their sense of gratification. As they keep potential consequences in mind, seeking alternative means and opportunities is never far from the forefront of their thinking process. The sociopath will for the most part still obtain what they desire, but more often than not they are more difficult to capture than psychopaths, as they tend to be careful not only in their planning and approach, but also in what traces of themselves they leave behind.

Many people will consider Ted Bundy, for instance, to have had a psychopathic nature. However, when we look at what he did, it would make more sense to label him a sociopath. He used the ruse of a broken arm to lure young girls to assist him at Lake Sammamish; when hunting girls outside of their sorority houses, he would pretend to drop his books while on crutches. Beyond that, Bundy to some extent altered his appearance in order to evade being recognised by potential eye-witnesses and authorities. While his crimes may have seemed psychopathic in nature in terms of their brutality and his own lack of remorse, his approach in terms of thinking could certainly be considered more sociopathic.

A certain amount of thought makes it clear that the sociopath would be the more dangerous of the two.

Nicolas continued to date the young nurse at the morgue; in turn, she went on exchanging sexual favours with Nicolas' boss so that he would pay for cosmetic surgery on her nose. Although Nicolas would only really meet with her on the weekends that he was left alone within the morgue, rumours had surfaced amongst the hospital staff that Nicolas and the young nurse had begun to see each other. In what seemed to be a coincidence, Nicolas was called to the hospital's Human Resources department and told that the morgue no longer required four persons to be on full-time duty there. As Nicolas was contracted to the morgue department, they were unable to remove him entirely from his duties. Therefore, Nicolas was told that he would now split his hours within the hospital between the morgue and the digestive system department, where he would act as a porter. Nicolas would work in the morgue during the mornings and then as a porter in the afternoons. He would still be required to work one out of every three weekends alone in the morgue.

Nicolas was convinced that this change to his duties within the hospital was not made out of necessity due to over-staffing at the morgue, but more out of a recommendation from the morgue boss, who was jealous of the relationship that Nicolas was having with the young nurse, especially as the young nurse was seeing Nicolas by choice, in complete contrast to his own situation with her. However, as Nicolas was contracted to the morgue, the very best that the boss was able to do was to have Nicolas removed for half of the time he was working in the hospital.

The idea of this infuriated Nicolas – so much so that he wished more than anything to get rid of the boss once and for all. Of course, Nicolas still wanted to get rid of all three of the morgue personnel, recalling the incident at the apartment of one of his co-workers when he had plotted to kill his colleague but had decided to refrain owing to the fact that he was a fellow 'Death Worker'. After his meeting with human resources, Nicolas began to regret not carrying out this killing, as it would have been one step closer to ridding himself of all three of the colleagues that he did not like.

While Nicolas was plotting on how to get rid of the three morgue workers, he began his new role within the digestive system department. In the afternoons away from his duties within the morgue, Nicolas was responsible both for wheeling patients to the surgery rooms for their operations and for cleaning the surgery rooms once the operation had been completed. There was always a large degree of blood splatter on the floor and walls, and it was also Nicolas' responsibility to clean these up. Further to this, Nicolas would obtain blood from the blood bank which would be used in any transfusions required during the surgeries. For example, should the surgeon estimate that four blood bags would be required for the forthcoming surgery, then Nicolas would bring the four bags as instructed; as each bag was used, a protective sticker would be removed and brought back to the blood bank offices. Therefore, if only three of the four bags were actually used, then three stickers would be removed, and along with the unused blood bag, they would be returned to the blood bank.

Nicolas spotted an opportunity – a means to acquire blood bags that were not used for the surgery. Should only three of the four potentially required blood bags get used in surgery, Nicolas would remove *all* the stickers from the bags and return them to the blood bank, stashing away the unused fourth bag for himself. He would hide the unused blood in his bag and at the end of his shift he would take the full blood bag home with him.

When blood is donated, it is separated into two different parts. The plasma is separated from the whole blood, and kept separate, while the red blood cells are kept in another bag. This process is called 'blood fractioning'. Different sections of the blood are used for different things during surgery. Plasma is the main clotting component of haemoglobin, as well as being the main transporters of glucose and other substances within the blood, whereas red blood cells mainly transport oxygenated blood to required areas and tissues within the body.

Nicolas would sometimes steal up to two or three bags of blood each week. He would try to obtain the bags which contained the red blood cells, as this was made up of a more consistent liquid, while the plasma bags had a tendency to congeal rather quickly

Nicolas would smear the entirety of his body with the red blood bags that he brought home. He would drink the blood as well. Incidentally, Nicolas has stated that red blood cells have a completely different taste than whole blood, which is all he had tasted up until that point. He would mix the stolen blood with the ashes that he had obtained from the stolen urns into his protein milkshakes. (Nicolas was still working out with weights at that point.) In truth, as well as obtaining a feeling of power from drinking the blood, he actually liked the taste. As such, he drank blood on a regular basis.

The more that Nicolas worked, the more that he would steal the unused blood from the blood bank. He craved the blood and the energy that it seemed to provide him with. This lead to a situation when, at one point, Nicolas had at least 10 bags of stolen blood in the fridge in his apartment. For Nicolas, this felt such a natural thing that he would sit and watch S&M video tapes in his living room, all the while sipping blood direct from the stolen bags as he watched, or he would make himself a cocktail of the blood mixed in with the ashes and casually watch his videos.

As was the case with all things in Nicolas' life, things began to escalate. He was quite content with drinking blood and cremation ashes, but in truth the more power and energy that he gained from his escapades, the more he was inclined to experiment further. One afternoon, when he was required to clean the surgery room within the hospital following a routine operation, Nicolas noticed that there were pieces of flesh in the drains and on the operating table which had been removed from a person during surgery. As there was no one else in the room to observe what Nicolas was doing, Nicolas picked up the pieces of flesh that he discovered and decided to satisfy his curiosity. He picked up the pieces of flesh and ate them raw, right there in the surgery room. This was the very first time that Nicolas tasted human meat, but it would not be the last.

When Nicolas was alone in the morgue, particularly at weekends, he would begin to take flesh from the bodies after the autopsies had been completed. Prior to stitching up the Y-shaped incisions on the body's torso, he would take a scalpel and remove sections of human meat. He would remove long thin strips, which he thought of as 'steak', from the ribcage and place them into plastic bags in order to take them home to eat.

Nicolas found that the ribcage area was the best area from which to remove pieces of flesh, as the deceased person would then be sewn up, thus eliminating the possibility that his tampering would be detected. However, while Nicolas enjoyed the sensation of eating human meat from the ribcage, he found that the meat taken from the back of the calf was more suitable for consumption.

Nicolas would take all the meat that he could and place them into plastic bags, so that he could store them in his fridge and eat them as and when he had the desire to do so. He would quite often mix the flesh from the morgue with the blood from the bags that he had stolen from the surgeries. As this was all new to Nicolas, it involved a great degree of experimentation.

Nicolas combined the human flesh in with the things that he would regularly have for his dinner, such as mashed potatoes and different sauces, as well as mixing the flesh in with regular meat that he had purchased from the supermarkets. Nicolas would take very thin slices of the human flesh and cook them in a pan for no longer than one or two minutes, cooking them in the same manner as he would do his regular favourite cut of beef steak. He would follow this recipe to the letter, except of course that he would replace the beef with thin slices of human flesh. He went as far as to serve them with side dishes such as chips.

Visually, these cuts of human flesh looked very similar to ordinary thin-cut steaks. As with regular beef steaks, Nicolas loved to cook them to the point that they melted onto his tongue. He would take a bite of the human flesh and leave it on his tongue, savouring the taste and sensation. Nicolas describes the taste of these steaks to be similar to horse, or even certain types of deer meat. However, unlike any of these animal meats, human flesh left a metallic taste in the mouth once the initial taste had passed.

As he did with other meats, Nicolas would remove all of the fat tissue from the human flesh before cooking and consuming it. He would do this by taking a razor blade and carefully removing any fat layers that he found there. In retrospect, though, Nicolas has stated that he would have preferred to have left the fat tissue on the meat, so as to enhance the taste of the meat.

Nicolas found all aspects of what he was doing to be extremely interesting. He wanted to make the human flesh that he was eating perfect – almost as if to prepare the 'meat' in a gourmet style, in keeping with France's reputation for fine cuisine. As time went on, Nicolas adapted his consumption of the flesh in a more sophisticated manner. However, when he initially ate the meat within the walls of the surgery room, he did it purely for the sensation of taking human flesh into his body. Despite the sophistication of his consumption methods as time went on, Nicolas' primary goal was to obtain that feeling of energy that he had when he consumed human flesh. The sensation was not dissimilar to the feeling he had when he consumed blood or ashes mixed in with his milkshakes, as though the taking in of human flesh seemed to elevate his feelings of power and energy. Nicolas has described the spiritual sensation of consuming human flesh as similar to that of a person taking a large amount of high-strength cocaine. The energy and power that he felt rush through his body when he consumed human flesh seemed to boost these feelings to an unprecedented scale. It was as though, with each sip of blood, each intake of cremation ashes and each morsel of human flesh that he digested, he gained the power of the dead, almost as a way of infusing this power into his own life-force.

Nicolas always took great care to ensure that he was never caught red-handed. Nicolas did not act on impulse, and as a result of this, was not hampered by his urges dictating his actions. Nicolas was methodical in his approach to all of his endeavours. He stole blood when he knew it was safe to do so; he took meat from the deceased bodies in the morgue when no one was around him; and, most importantly, he never told anyone what exactly he was doing. He never brought people back to his apartment, therefore there was never anyone in a position to inform any member of the authorities what it was that he was getting up to.

At this time, Nicolas, having moved out from the apartment in which he shared with his father, had moved to his own small apartment in Rue Coustou in the Pigalle district. His mother, who had been living in that very same area with her younger partner, had since separated from this partner and moved back into Nicolas' father's home, albeit into a separate bedroom. His parents never came to visit him at his new apartment: as a result, Nicolas was able to store the bags of stolen blood and the plastic bags containing human flesh in his fridge without fear of these being discovered by anyone other than himself.

As Nicolas now had his own apartment, he was free to do whatever he wished within the walls of his own home. He decorated the walls with posters of horror films, as well as various pictures with an S&M theme. Further to this, Nicolas was able to decorate the apartment with the bones that he had taken from cemeteries, along with the glass jars containing the remains of aborted foetuses that he had stolen from the St Vincent de Paul hospital. The apartment had a fold-down sofa bed: this, of course, served primarily as Nicolas' sleeping place, but in addition, Nicolas used it to store the guns which he had stolen from the military.

In his new apartment, Nicolas reconstructed the altar which he had previously set up in his father's basement. This was decorated with the human skulls and bones that he had obtained from breaking into mausoleums and crypts. His apartment would perhaps be less shocking by today's standards. However, during the 1990s, it would have been deemed similar to something out of a horror movie: shockingly so, considering that the apartment was decorated in not only the foetus jars and human bones. It would certainly have been deemed to have had a 'heavy' atmosphere, with things such as autopsy tools stolen from the morgue, hardcore S&M videotapes, autopsy manuals, cremation urns from the cemeteries, his vast true crime collection, not to mention the stolen human flesh and blood bags from the hospital. All this made Nicolas' apartment seem to be highly macabre, with an extremely unique aura. In the history of the households of true crime perpetrators, Nicolas' apartment is perhaps matched in terms of grimness only by Jeffrey Dahmer's, though that would have held that title purely for what was found in his fridge rather than for the décor.

Nicolas was proud of his apartment and the aura that it held. In Nicolas' mind, his apartment was far darker than Dahmer's, an opinion confirmed by the fact that when Nicolas was arrested some years later, a seasoned veteran of the police force in France was forced to take time off active duty owing to a form of PTSD, after having to witness what was discovered inside Nicolas' living quarters.

Nicolas was in his element, having discovered the freedom to engage in whatever activities that he liked, without having to conceal what he was doing from, say, his father. There was no longer any need to keep his items in a secret locked basement. Not only were the contents of his fridge 'safe' – despite comprising approximately 50 percent normal food and 50 per cent human flesh and stockpiled blood bags – because no one was there to investigate it, but Nicolas also felt free in his plans to experiment.

Out of interest, Nicolas would take one of the skulls that he had obtained from a cemetery, place it in his shower and proceed to pour a bag of blood over the skull, just to find out what it looked like. Nicolas loved the visual aspects of the blood-covered skull. He was very proud of this activity; these days he declares that had today's social media platforms existed then, he would most certainly have placed photographs of his artforms on sites like Instagram. He acknowledges that such an act would of course have drawn unwanted attention to himself, but while he has always paid careful attention to keep his activities below any form of radar, he points out with sincere honesty that he has always found a way to 'fuck it up' for himself by engaging in side-activities which always thrust him into the limelight.

The time that Nicolas lived in the apartment in the Pigalle district was, in his words, action-packed. In the apartment Nicolas would pray and meditate in front of his altar. He would offer prayers up to Pazuzu and Kali, as well as other demons. Outside of the apartment, the Pigalle district was packed with sex shops, where he would constantly be on the search for extreme S&M tapes. He was on a mission to find the elusive 'snuff film' that had, up until this point, been impossible to locate.

Living on his own, Nicolas was free to travel as much as he liked in his spare time, therefore short trips to places such as Amsterdam became a regular occurrence. In Amsterdam, in particular, Nicolas would peruse the vast amount of sex shops there, as ever trying to find snuff films. He would ask in as many shops as he could; however, because he was still so young, he tended to be dismissed by many of the shop owners and workers. What he was able to locate, though, was a film called *Pain 9*. This was one of a series of videotapes that involved a female drug addict, who had agreed to be filmed receiving pain and punishment in return for money for drugs. In the video Nicolas saw the woman being tortured in an extreme manner: she was whipped until she bled, while hooks were placed in sensitive parts of her body such as her labia. Nicolas recalls that even though the woman was desperate for money, it was clear that she did not enjoy any of the sufferings that she was subjected to.

Further to this, Nicolas discovered a form of Japanese anime called *Eroguro* – an abbreviation of the English words 'erotic grotesque'. The anime, in a manga style, showed people being raped by demons in hell, in a mixture of pornography, the macabre and demonic torture. The *Eroguro* was available as a series of videotapes as well as in magazine format. These days, with the use of the internet, it would be easy to find all manner of this type of material, but then it was extremely rare, and available only to a select, persevering audience.

Following one trip to Amsterdam, Nicolas had the idea of filming his very own snuff movie. After giving the subject a great deal of thought, he realised that the morgue would make the ideal setting for such a film. Apart from anything else, it offered the perfect environment for disposing of any bodies afterwards. He would have access to all manner of surgical tools, which, once he had completed his snuff movie, could be used to cut up the bodies. He could then seal the parts in special containers, which could then be sent to the crematorium for immediate disposal. No one would ever have known what had taken place. Indeed, Nicolas had heard rumours – rumours which incidentally he would later discover to be true – that gangsters would pay morgue technicians to dispose of victims of gangland slayings in exactly this manner. It even seemed to be a lucrative business, with morgue technicians paid good money to dispose of up to three or four bodies each year. While Nicolas liked the idea of using this method for his snuff films, he did not like the idea of being involved with this particular type of mobster. Not only would there be the constant threat of gangland connection, but there also seemed to be very little honour amongst these men, who used a kind of crime pyramid to do as they pleased. They extorted people and committed rape like other sects of the criminal underworld; however, for Nicolas these mobsters seemed to be nothing more than rapists with connections.

Rather than engage with any form of mobsters, Nicolas decided that he would make his snuff film by himself and dispose of the body without outside help. Nicolas began to plan out what he would like to do and decided that the thing that would ultimately benefit him the most would be to get rid of his current work colleagues. More importantly, he wished to get rid of his morgue boss. After all, this man had seemingly taken away Nicolas' afternoons of working in the morgue by reporting to human resources that Nicolas was no longer required for morgue duty. Nicolas believed that his boss had been done this out of jealousy and that his decision had nothing to do with the morgue's true work requirements.

While Nicolas was plotting his eventual snuff movie involving his co-workers, he continued to work in his dual role at the hospital. He started to maintain something of a social life as well. Through a mutual friend who ran a death metal fanzine, Nicolas met a girl called Sophia, who worked as a professional dominatrix. At only 18, Sophia was four years younger than Nicolas, now aged 22. The two began to see each other and started a relationship. Nicolas has subsequently described Sophia as tall and beautiful, with large breasts. Her face was adorned with a lot of piercings; one piercing on her nose was connected to another on her ear by a chain. It was a look that Nicolas did not like at all – so much so that he refused to hold her hand in public, simply because of the chain. Other than that, however, Nicolas liked almost everything about the girl. She was into the same types of horror movies as Nicolas was, such as the *Hellraiser* movies. What Nicolas particularly liked about her was that it was not just the horror elements of the movies that appealed to her, but also the spiritual dimension underpinning them. This was in a very similar vein to his own feelings.

Sophia was the only girl that Nicolas ever brought to his apartment. After some time he developed a sufficient degree of trust with her that he felt comfortable enough to show her the bones and skulls that he had obtained from the cemeteries. However, he still did not feel comfortable enough to show her the jars which contained the aborted foetuses and the human flesh which he kept in his fridge. Sophia liked the concept of blood and as a result they would incorporate blood into their sex life. The pair would often smear their bodies in blood during sex and further to this they would often drink each other's blood during intercourse. In Sophia's job, she would be paid by her clients to dominate them sexually; however, in her personal life she liked to be submissive to Nicolas. The pair would engage in strangulation as a means of foreplay and also during intercourse itself. On one occasion, Nicolas was strangling her a little too hard, to the point that she fainted from a lack of oxygen – though the more Nicolas noticed that she was not able to breathe, the less he found that he was able to stop. As he took the girl closer to the point of ending her life, the higher his sex drive engaged and the less it seemed he was able to control himself. Sophia changed colour from a lack of oxygen and her body went limp. It was at this point that Nicolas realised that the girl was going to die and, in a moment of clarity, he stopped choking her. Eventually, Sophia came round, coughing profusely. This experience alarmed her a great deal and it was almost a week before she decided to contact Nicolas again.

After Nicolas had come so close to ending the girl's life, the pair decided to focus more on what he has subsequently termed 'blood play'. This involved actually cutting each other's skin with scalpels stolen from the hospital. Nicolas would lightly cut words into her body – not that this mattered to Nicolas, as he describes her body as being covered in 'shitty tattoos' anyway. Further to this, Nicolas would take her to the morgue on the weekends that he was working there alone and have sex with her in the morgue. This was not the same as with the young nurse; with her, he would engage in sexual activity in the offices. With Sophia, however, he would have sex with her on the morgue table, even taking things so far as to bring out a corpse from one of the morgue fridges and make her look at the deceased person while the pair had sex. On one occasion, he instructed Sophia to hold a corpse's hand.

From Nicolas' point of view, he had absolutely no emotional connection to Sophia. As far as he was concerned, the entire engagement was nothing more than sex and experimentation. The two did have a lot of things in common, but there was no more to the relationship: he did not see them as soulmates or anything similar. Nicolas trusted Sophia to a degree, but clearly not enough to show her the more secret items in his flat, such as the glass foetus jars or the human flesh which he kept in his fridge.

At this time, Nicolas would continue to meet up with the young nurse who worked at the hospital. However, Nicolas has described the young nurse as being very normal in comparison with Sophia. Therefore, the majority of his experimentation came from the relationship with Sophia. As a child, Nicolas had learned how to ride horses. For some reason he still had a riding crop, used to whip a horse to make it go faster. He decided to use the crop on Sophia. He would whip her frequently; on one occasion, he whipped her so hard that the crop broke from the sheer impact. Nicolas would also pierce her nipples, as Sophia seemed to enjoy this sensation. Sophia seemed to love the fact that she was so submissive with Nicolas, in stark contrast to her professional life, where she was a young deliverer of punishment to what sounded to Nicolas like creepy and perverted old men.

Nicolas seemed to revel in his role: his mind and energy were reaching new peaks that he could not calculate in his own mind. The role with his girlfriend, the drinking of blood and the consumption of human flesh took his energy and spiritual awakening to another level. His inner being was coming to the surface, so much so that it was taking over his life. Soon it would develop from his waking desires into his dreams and subsequently, into his state of reality. It was as though it was developing a life force of its own.

NINE

DEATH COMES TO US ALL

Though Not All Are Chosen to Walk with Death

THE LADY IN White, or La Dame Blanche in France, is a mythological figure derived from Celtic and European folklore and commonly associated with death, destruction and annihilation. The Lady in White is also variously known as the Dryad of Death, The Queen of the Dead and also as the 'Crone' form of the Goddess of Death.

This supernatural goddess has often been depicted in modern television and in a variety of literary forms dating as far back as the 1700s. In each portrayal she appears as a ghostly figure of mystique, who intervenes in stories of crimes and other subjects pertaining to the subject of death.

In folklore, the Lady in White has been reported as having made her presence known at a time when death has just occurred, or when someone is about to meet their end. In a manner of speaking, the Lady in White takes on a role in the same vein as the better-known figure of the 'Grim Reaper'. In appearance, though, she is in stark contrast to the Grim Reaper, who is always depicted as a tall, dark, shrouded figure wielding a scythe towards everyone for whom death is at hand. The Lady in white is typically described in quite the opposite way: dressed in completely white garments with a somewhat ghostly aspect. She is reported to have been sighted particularly at accidental deaths, murders and even suicides: any death, indeed, with an underlying theme of loss and betrayal.

Again contrary to the image of the Grim Reaper, who is associated with darkness, the Lady in White is reported to have been seen in the daylight as much as during the hours of the night. In addition, the Lady has been known to appear in photographs of family members who have either just lost a loved one, or are approaching their final moments of life themselves. While the Lady in White may not present as overpowering an image as that depicted by the Grim Reaper, hers is no less fraught with death and despair.

What may come as a surprise is that while the image of the Grim Reaper has become more recognisable as a stereotype in modern entertainment, the Lady in White has far deeper roots in folklore around the world. She has been known to have appeared throughout the ages within Europe when any connection has been made to death, with far-reaching similarities to countries in Africa, where local myths of sightings pertaining to death have been recorded.

It can be deduced that a person who surrounds themselves with death and revels in the mindset of the macabre would, therefore, relate more to the Lady in White than to any other figure stemming from folklore. It would seem fathomable that such a person would have an interest in the Lady in White: not only would their paths cross, but in truth their paths could become one and the same.

The thought of committing murder was becoming ever more prevalent in Nicolas' mind. From his very first fantasies of hunting down the children of his class with the sphere from the *Phantasm* movie in his youth, to the thought of obtaining a rifle and shooting students from the top of the main tower building on his university campus, the thoughts of taking lives had always been in the forefront of his mind.

Nicolas had stolen guns from his time in the military for this very purpose, yet up until this point he had found it exceedingly difficult to obtain ammunition for the stolen weapons. This nullified his ability to carry out his desires. However, a loophole in French gun law would soon change that. In France at the time, no firearms licence was required for weapons bought with the sole purpose of use in sports. As a result, all that was required to purchase these weapons was simply an identification card, along of course with the ability to pay for the firearm.

Nicolas, who did not wish to draw attention to himself, got his girlfriend Sophia to purchase him two weapons using her identification. He was able to obtain a sports .22 calibre handgun. Owing to its design, this gun had to be manually reloaded after a single shot: it did not have any form or magazine in where multiple bullets could be stored for continuous use. Further to this, and still under the ruse of buying for sports, Nicolas was able to get a Mossberg 12.76-gauge shotgun, again using Sophia's identification to do so.

The lack of restriction with regards to purchasing the weapons was reflected in the ability to purchase the ammunition for these weapons, where the law was equally relaxed. Therefore, Nicolas could and did obtain all the ammunition for these weapons that he could have possibly hoped for.

At the exact moment of obtaining the guns, Nicolas did not have a specific intention or target in mind for using them on, as he was still planning this in his mind. Ideally, Nicolas still wanted to obtain a sniper-style rifle for his intentions, or at least obtain ammunition for the Famas rifle; however, he was happy to have obtained the .22 and the shotgun and ammunition for them. Owing to the sports-style handles that they had, both of these weapons could easily be hidden under a long coat if required. This suited Nicolas, considering that he was never short of ideas of what he could do when it came to making use of all manner of weapons.

At the time, Nicolas had been studying the actions and methods of the French serial killer Remy Roy, known to the public as the 'Minitel Killer'. Roy used an early video dating service called Minitel to lure his victims under the pretext of advertisements offering them gay sex. After he was caught bludgeoning a victim to death with a hammer, Roy was arrested and put on trial. Nicolas was following his case with great interest.

Nicolas noticed that his professional dominatrix girlfriend was also using Minitel in order to secure her clients. He began to study what she was doing in order to obtain tips and understand how the process worked. Naturally, he did not tell his girlfriend what he was doing; instead, he studied how his girlfriend approached her potential clients and began to grasp the process.

Therefore, Nicolas soon knew how to contact the people that he needed to, understanding which sections he needed to look into. Further to this, he understood that, in order to maintain his own safety, he would have to make use of the advertisements from a computer at public places such as the library and make telephone calls from public phones, all so that none of the online links or phone calls could be connected to his own home in any way whatsoever.

With everything that was going on in Nicolas' mind, coupled with the information that was in the media at the time, Nicolas found himself in a constant state of bewilderment. It was very difficult for him to separate his fantasies from what was happening in his day-to-day life. His dreams began to feel like reality and, in truth, Nicolas found the separation between the two increasingly difficult. In particular, Nicolas' dreams became extremely vivid and lifelike, to the point that the sensations that he felt within his dreams seemed exactly the same as in reality. He remembers waking in the night from a dream in which he seemed to have contacted a person on Minitel, gone to their houses and then proceeded to shoot them. Placing his gun back into his trousers, Nicolas had the sensation of the hot barrel of the gun against his skin which seemed identical to the sensation of heat that he would have had in real life.

Nicolas must have had about three or four dreams of this nature, each one almost seeming real and carried out in what felt like slow motion. In some of the dreams he would struggle with a victim that he had encountered, with shots being fired up in the air and into a ceiling of the victim's apartment. Other dreams would feel as though he had pointed a gun at the victim's head; when a shot was fired, small drops of what he imagined to be blood flowed from the neck or head of the dream victim. In the dreams the victim would be bleeding and would fall to the floor as a result of the injuries that they had sustained.

Not all of the victims in the dreams had died, though in one dream set in a top-floor apartment in Paris, the victim had been bludgeoned with a hammer, which may or may not have been fatal: as this was just a dream, it was impossible to determine or even recall correctly what had taken place. Nicolas, though, does recall feeling the stark difference between the cold steel of the hammer against his skin when putting it back into his trousers and the hot steel of a recently used gun, which had been the weapon of choice within another dream.

All of the dreams were extremely vivid in nature, perhaps due to a combination of fantasies and Nicolas' consumption of dairy products before going to sleep. The dreams felt real, but when Nicolas woke the next day following the dreams, all that he could remember was the hot or cold sensations against his skin, the potential mess that the victims' injuries may have caused, or the fact that the victims were faceless to him and zero eye contact was made.

Whether because of the nature of his dreams, or the media

coverage surrounding other cases at the time, Nicolas made the conscious decision to rid himself of the .22 calibre sports handgun that he had obtained. Therefore, at the end of the summer of 1994, Nicolas decided to file off the gun's external serial number, take the gun apart and file off its inner serial number. (This number, incidentally, is what the police use to match ballistics when comparing bullet fragments with a suspected murder weapon.) He then disposed of the gun parts in various bins across the city. In Nicolas' dreams he had never used the shotgun that he had obtained; therefore he decided that there was no need to dispose of this gun. One thing that Nicolas recalled from his dreams was that, whether he utilised a hammer or a gun, he always aimed for the temple on the skull. This is where the skull is the thinnest: as a result, striking this would induce the most haemorrhaging, both externally and internally.

The killer within Nicolas was beginning to emerge to the forefront of his mind. It was at this time, therefore, that Nicolas decided to get another tattoo which he felt represented his state of mind. He decided to get the words 'Serial Killer' inked onto his body, with the word 'Serial' tattooed on the back of his triceps on one arm and the word 'Killer' tattooed onto the same location on the other arm. This concept served in his mind to bring his innermost thoughts to the surface. It seemed as though the permanent marking on his skin of his inner traits would spur him into the planning stages of action, having broken free from not only his dreams, but, further still, from the shackles of his mind.

At this time, Nicolas' mind was spiralling out of control: it was increasingly difficult to disentangle his dreams from his waking sensations. As a result, he was harvesting feelings of craziness, anger and remorse. Nicolas had purchased a Pitbull dog – a red-nosed Pitbull – and when he came home from work one day, he had noticed that the dog had destroyed part of his apartment and made a mess everywhere. In a fit of rage, Nicolas grabbed hold of the dog and strangled it, eventually killing the dog.

Nicolas felt immediate remorse for his actions. It reminded him of a time when he was a child, living in Africa: his father had taken in a stray dog which had been coming to the house in search of food. The family kept the dog for approximately six months, up until the point that it was blamed for killing a sheep that belonged to one of the local tribesmen. As a result, the dog was destroyed and in accordance with local custom, its corpse was hung up and displayed in the centre of the town for all to see. Nicolas remembers feeling sorry for the dog. Although his father tried to comfort Nicolas, saying that he had had no option other than to comply with the local tribesmen, this did little to satisfy Nicolas' mind. The killing of his own dog now brought back all of these feelings within himself, even though he had been the one who was responsible this time. The feelings of sadness and remorse for the dog caused Nicolas to feel even angrier, thus making the series of negative emotions spiral into an apparently never-ending circle. Nicolas has described animals as innocents; therefore, the degree of remorse connected to the death of a pet is potentially unlimited.

The combination of mixed emotions within Nicolas at this point in time – the vividness and reality of his dreams, combined with the energy and power that he felt from drinking blood and feasting on human flesh – caused Nicolas' sexual desires to go into overdrive. His sex drive was becoming stronger and stronger, and he felt as though he could not contain it from going beyond a reasonable limit. Nicolas wanted sex all the time, whether from the nurse he would meet on the weekends in the morgue, or from the dominatrix girlfriend he was seeing during the week. The increase in his sex drive lead to him using more and more toys and equipment when his girlfriend was being submissive to him. In addition to his riding crop, he incorporated things such as paddles and spiked wheels (specifically designed for S&M) into their sex life.

Nicolas gained a love of using toys during sex, as well as a thirst to continue incorporating blood into their acts.

Nicolas was becoming paranoid though about the use of blood: he was, after all, stealing the blood from the hospital. As such, how he had obtained the blood was a secret, a secret that he did not feel comfortable sharing with his girlfriend. However, it was as though he felt he was trapped in a vicious circle: despite the sense of paranoia about his secrets being exposed, the consumption of human flesh and blood served only to increase his desire to want more. Nicolas was obsessed with this consumption, not dissimilar to the characters portrayed by Guy Pearce and Robert Carlyle in the 1990s movie *Ravenous*. (Incidentally, he would be gifted a DVD of this film by serial killer Remy Roy in prison at a later date.)

One of Nicolas' friends, named Christo, noticed that Nicolas seemed to be becoming more and more on edge. Christo suggested taking Nicolas off to Poland for a vacation for a short while, hoping that the change of scenery would perhaps calm him somewhat. Nicolas obliged; however, while this was meant to be a relaxing vacation, Nicolas saw this as a means by which he could obtain ammunition for his Famas rifle in one of the Eastern European black markets which were in abundance at the time. (Such markets do not exist today; however, as eastern Poland had links to Russia at the time, it was easier to obtain such things from across the border.) Nicolas describes Poland at this time as being similar to the Wild West: a place where people could obtain things such as ammunition and vast amounts of illegal drugs without difficulty.

The pair slept in people's so-called 'dens'. One of the dens they stayed at would become famous: it was owned by a musician who later became prominent in the Polish Black Metal music scene. As part of their Polish excursion, they were taken to see the notorious death camps of World War II, such as Auschwitz-Birkenau and Treblinka. At these places, Nicolas would recall feeling emotions similar to the sensations of vibrating that he had first felt in 1982, at the funeral home where his grandfather had been laid out, in the small coastal town in Brittany. This was part of a trend which seems to have followed Nicolas at any place of death that he has visited in his life: a sensation of energy that he himself is finely attuned to, almost as though he can home in on the energy of death, regardless of the place or time, regardless of whether anyone else is in sync with these feelings: almost as though the dead, through a series of vibrations, can communicate with him on a level different from any other.

The vacation to Poland did little to ease the connection with death that Nicolas seemed to have. On his return to the morgue, Nicolas began plotting how to remove the co-workers of the morgue, as well as his jealous boss. Nicolas thought about bringing a gun to work and shooting each of them as they entered the building. Nicolas understood, though, that this would have been acting on impulse: as a result, it was almost certain that he would have been arrested for his actions. Therefore, he had mixed feelings about what to do next.

Nicolas had managed to obtain another .22 calibre handgun. This time he did not use his girlfriend's identification, but instead managed to persuade the girlfriend of one of his friends to use her ID to purchase the gun. This handgun was similar to the one he previously owned, with the same mechanism for reloading after every shot. Nicolas began to carry the new handgun with him at times: this seemed to increase his feelings of power, so much so that when Nicolas found himself in the morgue on his own, he would walk up to the chapel connected to the morgue, take out the gun and point it at the figure of Christ, taking aim at the head.

In the time that followed, Nicolas found himself seeing his girlfriend Sophia less and less frequently. In the past he had met up with her at least three or four times a week; however, she made the claim that she was becoming busier with her client list and as a result he began to see her only once a week. In addition to this, Nicolas was called to the hospital's human resources office as his initial 10-month contract was up. HR stated to him that there was no longer a requirement for four people to be employed within the morgue. As a result, Nicolas was offered a full-time position in the digestive system department of the hospital, the same department where he had been working in the afternoons. HR stated to him that should there be a requirement in the future for further staff in the morgue, then he would naturally be the first person that they consider. However, Nicolas knew that this would not be the case: he understood that his ousting from the morgue was due to jealousy from the boss and as such, his chances of being recalled to morgue duties were almost non-existent. As a result, and to the complete surprise of HR, Nicolas refused the position that he was offered. Despite HR's attempts to retain his services, especially because he was deemed to be a good worker, Nicolas decided to leave.

On his last day in the morgue, Nicolas was left alone to carry out his duties. He had in his possession the key to the morgue: during his lunch break, he went to the local locksmiths and had the key cut and copied. By doing so, Nicolas would be able to access the morgue and when the time was right, perhaps a few months later, he would lie in wait within the morgue and ambush his former colleagues one by one as they entered the building. Further to this, Nicolas planned to ritualise the killings of his former colleagues by keeping the severed heads of their corpses in the morgue fridges – having severed the heads himself – and then placing the heads in a ritualistic circle around himself on the floor of the morgue.

A few days after leaving the morgue, Nicolas was anxious to get himself a job at another morgue within Paris. Therefore, Nicolas, just as he had done when he first left University, sent out an abundance of CVs to all the hospitals within the region. The difference this time was that the replies were not as quick as he had hoped for. He had even sent a letter to the city morgue, which dealt primarily with the bodies of people who had been either murdered or involved in fatal accidents. Nicolas' ideal of working in a morgue where his potential victims might have ended up appealed to Nicolas. However, at this time the city morgue did not answer. (However, they would contact Nicolas in the years to come, but he declined: given his past and the morgue's access to police files, it would have drawn unnecessary attention to him.)

Following his departure from the morgue, Nicolas decided to rid himself of the weapons that he had stolen during his military service. As he had done with his previous .22 calibre gun, Nicolas dismantled the guns and filed the serial numbers off before disposing of the gun sections in various places across the city. Up until this point, he had not been able to obtain ammunition for these guns; nevertheless, despite this he thought it was in his best interests to rid himself of them. This was a decision, however, that he came to regret the very next day: his mind was extremely chaotic at that point in time, and he felt as though it was the best thing to do. This revelation would actually come to serve him as a positive move a little later down the line.

October 4th, 1994

On the morning of October 4th, 1994, Nicolas went to the public library in the 15th District of Paris. While in the library, Nicolas used the library computer to log onto the BDSM section of Minitel. On Minitel he discovered an advertisement for a man who was looking for another male willing to inflict severe punishment on him. Having obtained the telephone number for the man, he phoned him from a public telephone in this district and arranged to meet him at noon at the man's home.

Nicolas took his newly acquired .22 gun, gloves, rope, plastic bags and a large butcher's knife and placed them into his bag, surrounded by a few T-shirts so that they would not rattle against each other and alert anyone as to this additional noise. The man's house was in the 12th District of Paris and to get there Nicolas would need to take the subway. He was wearing surgical gloves which he had taken from the hospital where he had been working; over these he had placed black leather gloves. Nicolas was dressed entirely in black, other than his favourite jacket – a beige Carhartt jacket, which was also worn by the protagonist of the infamous film *Henry: Portrait of a Serial Killer*.

At noon, Nicolas arrived at the subway stop Filles du Calvaire ('Daughters of Calvary' in English) and went to the man's home. During the time that Nicolas was walking to the man's home, he was thinking about how good his new gun would be when used at point-blank range. This type of gun was known as a good sports weapon, used at a distance: Nicolas knew that the velocity of the bullet fired from the gun would increase over distance and that there were doubts as to its effectiveness at short or point-blank range.

Nicolas brought a knife with him not out of any desire in order to dismember any bodies but merely as a backup weapon should the gun prove to be of no use at short range. In truth, Nicolas did not care who the person was that he was going to shoot: what mattered to him was the usefulness of his gun and whether or not it would be effective enough for Nicolas to use again in the future.

Nicolas arrived at the man's apartment, which was located on the fourth or fifth floor. The building was old and as a result it had no elevator; therefore, Nicolas had to climb the stairs up to the man's apartment. No one saw him going up the stairs, mainly because it was during the middle of the day and most of the people living in the building would have been either at work or at school.

Nicolas arrived at the man's front door and proceeded to knock on the door. The door opened and a man who was slightly taller than Nicolas opened the door. Nicolas does not remember what this man's face looked like, although he does remember that the man was dressed entirely in white, while Nicolas was dressed the opposite, in nearly all black clothing. Nicolas recalls that the fact that the man was dressed in completely white attire seemed to be strange; however, when Nicolas imagined what the man's white clothing would look like covered in blood, he thought that this would be 'cool'.

The two of them went inside the apartment. Strangely enough, no words were exchanged between the two. They took three steps in, and as the man was closing the door behind Nicolas, Nicolas took the gun from out of his bag and aimed it at the man's face. As the man turned around and saw Nicolas pointing a gun in his face, he seemed to be startled and surprised: this was not what he was expecting Nicolas to be there for.

Nicolas pulled the trigger from no more than a few paces away. The bullet entered the man's body through the right eye socket. From what Nicolas was later told, the bullet stopped in its tracks just short of the base of the brain, subsequently causing a haemorrhage in the man's head. The man fell face-first onto the floor. At the time, Nicolas would recall, his pulse seemed to slow in pace, and it was almost as though he could feel himself standing outside his own body, staring at the carnage that was unfolding before him. It was as though Nicolas was a spectator, watching himself shoot the man.

The man was still on the floor, face down and twitching as he tried to produce any form of movement. Nicolas remained as cool as ice, not reacting to any of the man's movements; instead, he was listening to whether anyone was coming as a result of hearing the sound of the gun going off. But there was none: the sound of the gun, being a .22 calibre, was not as loud as one would think. In fact, the sound of the gun going off could be likened to that of someone slamming a door loudly.

Nicolas walked around the man's apartment and down the corridor as he reloaded the gun. He noticed that there were jazz posters on the wall; more specifically, they were jazz posters of a festival where the man had been working as a musician. The man began to make squeaking noises. Nicolas observed him and noticed that blood had begun to pool around his head as he lay on the floor. However, owing to the amount of blood that Nicolas could see, he knew that the initial bullet had done its job and that the man would die as a result of the gunshot wound. Nicolas did not feel rushed to get on with what he had come there for; instead, he walked into the man's kitchen and opened the fridge. To his surprise, Nicolas noted that all that the man had in his fridge were some chocolate chip cookies, a bottle of tomato ketchup and a bottle of mayonnaise. Nicolas took the cookies and started eating them as he walked around the apartment. Nicolas then sat in a chair eating the cookies as he watched the man slowly dying.

To Nicolas, it was quite a spiritual experience. He wanted to savour the moment of taking the man's life and watch the man's soul leaving his body. By being present at the time of death, Nicolas wanted to feed on the soul of the man as a psychic vampire would have done. Later, when questioned whether he drank the man's blood, Nicolas would confirm that he didn't. Given Nicolas' later reputation, people would misunderstand the function of the knife as part of the killing: for Nicolas, the knife was brought as a backup, not to cut the man's body to take blood or even to eat his flesh.

During the 1990s, AIDS was a terrifying epidemic across the world: because Nicolas' victim had led a homosexual lifestyle, the possibility of contracting AIDS from the man's blood was a concern. However, the killing itself had nothing to do with a hate crime against gay men, and Nicolas states that his thoughts would have been the same if the person had been female. The human flesh and blood that Nicolas had taken from the hospital and consumed had either had a case file or blood reports done on them and therefore was tested for diseases. As a result, Nicolas understood that the flesh and blood were safe, but could not say the same about this man's body.

(A side note that should be mentioned in terms of understanding the concept of AIDS at the time is that Jeffrey Dahmer would actually use a condom when having sex with corpses in the late 1980s and early '90s, such was his fear of contracting the virus.)

Nicolas got up from the chair and tapped the man on the back of the head with the barrel of the gun – not in a violent manner, but more to see what the man's current state was at the time. Nicolas tried to move the man's head with the barrel of the gun so that he could see the gunshot wound for himself, but the man's head had become stuck to the floor from all the blood that had poured out from the wound. Nicolas knew that the man was still not dead; however, the man no longer seemed to have any sense of what was happening. Nicolas was enjoying watching the death process. As the red pool of blood was gathering even more under the fallen man, Nicolas readied himself to shoot again with the reloaded gun. He took aim at the back of the man's head and pulled the trigger once again. A spurt of blood emitted from the back of the man's head and seemed to stain the white shirt that he was wearing, turning it red. Following the second gunshot, the man shivered and made a few more barely discernible noises.

Nicolas reloaded the gun again and shot the man for a third time. This time he aimed the gun into the man's back, where Nicolas envisaged where the heart would be. Yet another red stain of blood filled the white-coloured shirt that the man was wearing. When Nicolas listened to the noise the man was making, he heard that he was breathing quite chaotically. Nicolas understood that the bullet had not hit the man in the heart, but in fact had punctured the man's lung.

Nicolas continued to eat the chocolate cookies as he watched the man slowly die. Nicolas was observing his movements closely, as the entirety of the experience was like a religious experience to him. Nicolas began meditating. As he was doing so, he watched the blood splatters on the man's white shirt form patterns, much as one would do when trying to form patterns from clouds in the sky.

The man was now beginning to cough up blood. As yet there were still no sounds from outside of the apartment. Nicolas was not feeling any forms of stress, and therefore he decided to take his time with the entire experience. He was there approximately half an hour in total. By contrast, the attacks that Nicolas had committed in his dreams prior to this point in time felt as if they had only taken about 10 minutes, from what Nicolas would later recall. With the events that were happening in the apartment, Nicolas felt relaxed, comfortable and took the time to enjoy the experience without the feeling of becoming stressed. He was at complete ease.

After a while, Nicolas heard footsteps outside the apartment. It was as though the footsteps that he heard were ones of those of a person who was leaving the building at a fast rate. Nicolas no longer began to feel safe within the confines of the man's apartment and understood that it was time to leave the building. However, at that point in time, the man on the floor was still not dead. According the autopsy reports later on, the man was shot a total of five times. However, Nicolas cannot recall the exact number of times he pulled the trigger, as the experience for him was not about seeing how many times he could shoot the man, it was more about experiencing the man die in front of him. Nicolas could see that although the man was certainly going to die, he was not going to die right away. Therefore, he decided to assist the man to reach the light at the end of the tunnel.

Nicolas found a large flowerpot inside the apartment. The pot was filled with soil; there were no plants in it. Nicolas raised the flowerpot above his head and brought the heavy pot crushing down onto the dying man's skull. He heard a loud cracking noise and Nicolas understood that the sound comprised not only the pot breaking, but also the skull being crushed under the pot's weight. The man ceased to move; he was finally dead. Nicolas looked closely at the bullet wounds, as if he would somehow be able to see light radiating from the holes that the .22 gun had created – as if the man's life force would emanate from any of the wounds. Nicolas did not see anything. There was just stillness.

The clothes Nicolas was wearing during the murder
(now displayed in Last Dime Museum, Indiana, USA)

As the man lay dead on the floor of his own apartment, Nicolas looked around the room one last time. He wanted a souvenir of his exploits: in the end, he found an answering machine, along with the man's wallet. Nicolas took both, not for their monetary value but as a token to remind him what he had done that day. He had wanted to take a piece of the man's blood-stained shirt but owing to the noise that the flowerpot had made when it came crashing down onto the man's skull, he no longer felt safe. Therefore, he took the answering machine and the man's wallet, placed them in his bag and proceeded to exit the apartment.

Nicolas made his way down the stairway of the building. As he passed the second floor of the building, he saw, out of the corner of his eye, a figure in white staring in his direction. He turned once again to see who it was that had been looking at him, but when he turned to gain a proper look, there was no one standing there.

Nicolas was certain that he had seen someone in white. To this day he is convinced that the person that was staring at him as he exited the building was the personification of death: rather than the Grim Reaper, this was the Lady in White, presenting herself at times of death and annihilation: *La Dame Blanche*.

TEN

CHAOS AND STRUCTURE

The Aftermath and Strategy

THE GAME OF chess can be a complicated one. Just as with other games of logic, a straightforward approach can sometimes be of great benefit to a participant and at other times it can leave a person at a severe disadvantage, outclassed by an opponent with a superior strategy. Of course, a daring move can pay off at certain moments within the game, whereas too bold a move at other times can leave a player open to risk and ultimately leave what was a position of strength looking extremely vulnerable. It is not a case of merely playing by the rules, but more how much a person is willing to risk playing within the rules and whether their gamble ultimately leaves them either in a position of triumph or looking back at how they could have done things differently.

At times, the outcome of the game relies not only on a person's own ability but also, in part, being able to determine both the skill and the predictability of an opponent and having the foresight and awareness to be able to anticipate that opponent's next move.

Ultimately, life is no different, metaphorically speaking, to that of a game of chess. A person will make their own moves, to try to predict the moves of others and in the end a skilled person will be able to anticipate the strategy and predictability of others in order to strengthen their own position. Life is a game of politics, strategy and perception. It begins in school and rears its head in adolescence; the moves and strategy that you employ will determine your overall standing, whether it be in the workplace, social circles, or even political surroundings. Institutions such as the army and prison will make this more evident: the personal standing of a person, whether they are strong or weak, will be highlighted in such a concentrated environment. Chess is strategy, as is life. It is the implementation of the ideas of Darwin: the survival of the fittest (body or mind) takes prevalence in our carnal society, with the ability to predict the actions of others giving a person their ultimate advantage.

After he had shot and killed the man in his apartment in the Filles du Calvaire area and had seen, or thought he had seen, the 'Lady in White', Nicolas continued down the stairs and made his way onto the open street. He returned to his apartment in the Pigalle district of Paris, complete with the souvenirs of his exploits. Once home, he opted to not rid himself of the .22 calibre gun that he had just used as the murder weapon; instead, he placed the gun underneath his bed once again. Nicolas took his souvenirs from his bag and decided that he would plug the answering machine into his own phone and use the machine for himself.

On inspection of the deceased man's wallet, Nicolas noticed that there were several items inside the wallet that could be of further use to him: the man's driving licence and an unused, blank cheque. Nicolas decided to purchase a camcorder, so that he would be able to record any further exploits. In addition, a camcorder would be a significant trophy to serve as a reminder of what he had done that very afternoon. In order to validate any purchases made using the blank cheque in the deceased man's name, Nicolas opted to forge the man's ID by placing a picture of himself inside it. This would, he thought, remove any suspicion as to why he did not resemble the photograph on the driving licence.

Nicolas, however, was still feeling elated and possibly 'on a high' after returning home from the murder, As a result, when placing his own picture in place of the deceased man's photo, he did not notice how crude his alteration of the ID actually was. Seemingly oblivious as to the details of his forgery, Nicolas took the blank cheque and the modified ID to a local department store in the hopes of purchasing the camcorder. The model that Nicolas had in mind was one that was quite expensive in comparison to many others on the market at the time. At the department store Nicolas took the camcorder that he wished to have, along with the blank cheque and forged ID, and went up to the sales desk where he hoped to complete his purchase.

Upon arrival at the sales desk, when Nicolas presented the blank cheque and the ID to the sales assistant, the assistant took one look at the ID and knew immediately that it was forged. However, he did not let Nicolas know that he understood the ID to be a forgery and instead innocently told Nicolas that he had to make a routine photocopy of the ID as per the store's protocol and policy. Nicolas believed that this was a part of the process and as such, waited at the desk while the sales assistant tended to his duties. In the distance, Nicolas could see that the sales assistant was now speaking to the head of security and at that moment understood that if he was caught using a forged ID, he would be arrested. With his plans to obtain a new camcorder seemingly soured by the real-isation of the staff that the ID was a forgery, Nicolas decided to leave the department store before he could be arrested. In doing so, however, he left the blank cheque and the forged ID at the store, as both were still in the possession of the sales assistant.

Having left the department store, Nicolas did not think too much about the forged ID: as it was with all of his previous exploits, Nicolas felt that he was protected, spiritually and phys- ically. As Nicolas had not followed through with the purchase of the camcorder, he guessed that the sales assistant and the head of security would simply dispose of the items, as no sale had actu- ally taken place. Therefore, there had been no crime, nullifying any requirement to follow it up. Thoughts such as these were, naturally, delusional; however, Nicolas would later admit that, owing to his heightened state following the murder, his thought process at the time was not the clearest. He had been meticulous in his approach to the murder and the attention to detail in ensuring that he would not be caught. On the other hand, Nicolas readily admits that the manner in which he approached the aftermath was handled extremely poorly – almost the polar opposite in terms of attention to detail.

Following his failed attempt to obtain the camcorder, Nicolas returned to his apartment, where, over the next few days he would continue to watch the news and read the newspapers for any reports pertaining to the murder that he had committed in the Filles de Calvaire area.

He found no reports of his crime. However, what he did see was a story about two young punks which had taken place on the same day as his murder. This male and female couple, who had connec- tions to the criminal underworld, had stolen a car with the intent of robbing a grocery store. Following this, the pair had hijacked a taxi in order to make their getaway from the scene of the crime. The taxi driver, in an attempt to foil their plans, had deliberately crashed the taxi with all three occupants inside, into a police car at a part of Paris called Place de la Nation. After they got out of the crashed taxi, a gun battle ensued, in which five people died, including the taxi driver himself, the male would-be criminal and three police officers. The surviving female criminal, Florence Rey, became known as an infamous 'cop killer'. For a short period of time, it was suspected that the murder that Nicolas had committed was connected to the carnage that had taken place at the Place de la Nation. As such, with no news reports of anything to do with a forged ID, Nicolas assumed that the heat for his crime would be on the two assailants of the Florence Rey shootout. Of course, it was not.

As there was nothing in the news regarding his crime, or even the fake ID, Nicolas presumed that he had got away with his crime and therefore decided that there was no need for him to dispose of his gun. So he kept it, with the idea of looking for new targets to continue his death-related fantasies.

Weeks passed and still, there was no new information about his murder, with the majority of the news still remaining focused on the Florence Rey case. Nicolas had begun to resume his normal life and as such began to engage once more with social settings. On 31 October 1994, Nicolas attended a Halloween party held at a fetish club. At the party, revellers were making use of a prop coffin, taking ludicrous photographs of themselves posing with it. Nicolas, who was still committed to the idea that he was a 'death worker', found this to be insulting and indeed disrespectful toward his chosen trade. He was angry at the people in the fetish club and he would later remember that he wished to bring a gun there and shoot all those who, in his mind, he deemed to be unworthy of touching such a revered thing as a coffin.

Further to this, Nicolas had not forgotten about his former colleagues at St Joseph's morgue, whom he was planning to kill in the morgue and after doing so, to take their severed heads and place them in a ceremonial circle on the morgue floor. Nicolas went to the morgue on a weekend night, gaining access to the building using his copy of the morgue door key. He let himself into the building late at night and prepared to lie in wait for his former colleagues. During Nicolas' previous exploits, he had nearly always forgotten a vital piece of equipment – for instance, forgetting to bring a hacksaw with which to sever the head of the corpse in the Russian mausoleum – and this time Nicolas had forgotten to bring a torch with him. He had all the other equipment that he needed: the gloves, the gun, etc. However, as the morgue was plunged into darkness at night, he needed a torch in order to make his way around. Turning on the morgue lights was not an option, as doing so would have alerted any passers-by that someone was inside. Disappointed at forgetting this vital piece of equipment, Nicolas temporarily abandoned this plan, locking the doors to the morgue as he left – with the intention, however, of returning before Christmas, this time with all of the equipment that he required, to kill all three of his former colleagues.

As Nicolas was making his future plans for murder, what he did not realise was that the police were now actively looking for him. They had realised that the man that Nicolas had murdered was not connected with the Florence Rey shootings, having determined that the calibre of the gun that Nicolas had used was not the same as in the Place de la Nation shootings. Nicolas' use of the deceased man's ID card, with his own photograph added to it, meant that the police had a connection between Nicolas and the ID's owner. Nicolas' photograph had now been circulated to every single police station in Paris and, in turn, an active search for Nicolas had begun. They did not know the name of the person that they were looking for; other than the photograph on the forged ID, there were no other links to Nicolas at the time. Nicolas had made all his phone calls from public telephones and had always accessed the 'Minitel' platform via library computers. Therefore, there had been no active leads to help the police pursue Nicolas.

November 12th, 1994

Owing to the fact that Nicolas had not, to this point, seen his picture in any of the newspapers or on TV, he thought that he had gotten away with the murder in Filles du Calvaire. On the 12th of November, a Saturday, Nicolas decided to attend a rock concert at Club La Locomotive, which was directly opposite the famous Moulin Rouge Cabaret in the Pigalle district of Paris. He had been standing outside the club, where he was waiting for someone, when, out of nowhere, two men appeared and pushed Nicolas up against the wall of the club. Nicolas had his arms turned behind his back and subsequently handcuffed. Nicolas then heard one of the men speak into his radio, saying the words: 'We have got him!'

The official story that emerged was that these two men happened to be attending the concert at the club because the girlfriend of one of them was a member of the band scheduled to be playing there that evening. Both men were also off-duty police officers. As all police officers in Paris had been instructed to carry a copy of Nicolas' picture from the forged ID with them at all times, one of them had recognised Nicolas and decided to apprehend him. However, as Nicolas understands it, this was not the whole story: he believes that his 'friend' from the punk rock scene, who had worked in the gun shop, had led police to Nicolas' whereabouts in the hope of obtaining a reward, having seen Nicolas' picture after the police had circulated it around the gun shops of Paris in the hope of obtaining a potential lead.

Following his arrest, Nicolas was taken to the nearest police station. The arresting officers and the staff in attendance at the local station had been given strict instructions to not take any form of statement from Nicolas, or even to speak to him for that matter. After being detained for some time, Nicolas was taken to the now-famous *Brigade Criminelle*, located at 36 Quai des Orfèvres in Paris. This famous building has been called France's version of

London's Scotland Yard and has featured in many crime movies: true-crime buffs will recognise the name, as it was the place where previous criminals such as Issei Sagawa and Remy Roy were interrogated. The building itself is located near Notre Dame Cathedral.

Nicolas' mugshot

Nicolas was taken to the interrogation rooms at the very top of the building, near the rooftops. Nicolas recalls being marched up about four or five floors of stairs and remembers seeing what can only be described as 'suicide netting' along the stairs, placed there so that suspected criminals could not leap to their death from the stairs rather than being taken into custody by the police. Nicolas remembers having mixed feelings about walking up the stairs, as he understood that he was being taken somewhere special, as he had previously seen these stairs on TV. Naturally, he was depressed at having been apprehended; however, he recalls a sense of being 'wowed', as he understood that he was now entering the world of the extreme justice system.

Nicolas did not know exactly what time he was taken to the interrogation offices of the building but estimated it to be roughly 2 o'clock in the morning. There was one person in the room, who then handcuffed one of Nicolas' arms to a desk, leaving the remaining arm free so that Nicolas could sign any necessary paperwork – for example, a confession. A brief look around the room showed an array of computers, as well as numerous case files; at the time Nicolas did not know if these were in any way related to himself.

After handcuffing Nicolas to the desk, the interrogating officer said to Nicolas: 'I hope that you are not going to do anything foolish?' He then proceeded to ask Nicolas about the driving license.

Nicolas replied that he had found the license at the subway station and as a result he did not understand what all the fuss was about. The police officer asked Nicolas about the murder, to which Nicolas said that he did not understand how that could be connected to him in any way, as all that he had done was to find the driving license and proceed to forge it. He stated that he had nothing to do with any murder case.

At this point, the officer decided to send Nicolas to a cell. The officer required the remainder of the staff who had been working on the case to be present for the interrogation and owing to the fact that it was roughly 2 am at the time, it would be a while before the police were able to get them back into the office. Nicolas remained in his cell in the building for approximately six hours before being brought back into the interrogation offices. In the time leading up to his arrest, Nicolas did not actually think that he was going to be caught and as a result, he had no thoughts regarding consequences or even a backup strategy.

Regardless of whether he was able to conjure up a backup strategy, Nicolas understood that he was in deep water. He knew that the officers were going to search his apartment and would find the gun that he had used for the murder, as he had decided not to dispose of it. Nicolas was taken back to the office for interrogation. On the desk, photographs of the murder and crime scene were laid out in front of Nicolas to see. This is a common interrogation technique, which allows the police to gauge the response of the murder suspect. The thinking behind this is that if the murder suspect seems mesmerised rather than shocked at the sight of the crime, then it gives an indication that the suspect is indeed guilty of the crime. Further to the photographs, there were now approximately ten police officers now in attendance, and all seemed to be staring directly at Nicolas. Some would speak and others remained silent, all apparently going through the 'good cop – bad cop' routine. Nicolas was silent. He looked up at all of the officers who were staring at him, then after roughly ten minutes of nothing but staring at each other, Nicolas broke his silence and said: 'OK, I did it...'

Nicolas could see a light almost shine from the eyes of one of the officers, who in turn replied, 'You have just saved yourself a lot of very long years in prison by confessing.'

Nicolas then proceeded to tell his version of events regarding the murder. He stated that the day before the October 4th murder, he had been harassed by a gay man in the Père Lachaise cemetery, which he had deemed to be his own territory. Following the harassment, Nicolas wished to get revenge on the gay community by killing on their own territory, which he deemed to be the 'Minitel' dating service.

This confession led only to further questions, such as: 'Was this the first time that you have done this?'

Nicolas replied, 'Yes.'

The police were not convinced, as it transpired that they were investigating a series of homosexual murders involving the use of a .22 calibre gun and wanted to link them to Nicolas. These murders, incidentally, were not dissimilar to the vivid dreams that Nicolas had previously had.

Nicolas stated that the only other time that he had used the gun was for target shooting. However, the police were still not convinced. They tried to show Nicolas photographs of other crime scenes, but Nicolas did not respond in any way that would have given a notion of guilt. Nicolas had had dreams of further crimes, but these were just fantasies. Despite his dreams having some resemblance to the files and photos of other crime scenes, Nicolas chose his words very carefully, repeating his statement word for word and insisting that the only other shooting that he had done was for target practice. His tale of events made his story a sustainable one and despite what the officers wrote on their note-pads, Nicolas used his words with great caution, as though he were walking on eggshells.

There was nothing the police had that could link Nicolas to any other crimes other than the one that he had confessed to. Then, with the accompaniment of a court-appointed lawyer, the police took Nicolas to his apartment for a search of the premises. This is a mandatory part of the procedure and the court-appointed lawyer in attendance is required so that everything is seen to be done by the book, with no possibility of things such as the planting of evidence occurring.

On the way to Nicolas' apartment, he was driven in a car, complete with three police officers. On route to his apartment, the three officers were chatty with one another, speaking candidly about a party that one of them had attended the night previously. To the officers, this was thus far just another case, nothing out of the ordinary in terms of their day-to-day jobs.

By the time the car arrived at Nicolas' apartment, the road had been cordoned off by a series of other police cars. An officer took

Nicolas' keys and opened the door to his apartment. Once the door was opened, everyone went quiet. In Nicolas' words, they went *REALLY* quiet. Inside the apartment, the officers found the human skulls, the mobiles that Nicolas had constructed out of human bones, the urns that Nicolas had stolen from the crematorium, as well as the posters, books and videotapes which not only related to horror movies, but to extreme bondage and S&M culture. The police also discovered the human skull which Nicolas had drenched entirely in human blood, along with the glass jars which contained aborted foetuses. Then they opened Nicolas' fridge, which was filled with bags of blood and as yet unidentified sources of meat. One of the older policemen picked up one of the cremation urns and stated: 'This is really, really macabre. We are onto something else here entirely.'

There was a clear tension in the air, something that even the most experienced of police had not been subjected to before. It was a small apartment, and the tension of a small apartment filled with police was trumped only by the astonishment at what the police had discovered. Everything that Nicolas had collected in his apartment was confiscated (and destroyed after his trial). The flesh and the urns were taken so that DNA sampling could be done. The sampling of the urns – or, more to the point, the ashes within the urns – seemed to be a waste of time and money, as no DNA can be extracted from crematory ashes.

On the way back to the police headquarters, Nicolas rode alongside the exact same three officers who had driven him to his apartment, only this time the officers did not seem as buoyant or as talkative as they had been previously. They were silent, none of them willing to make any form of eye contact with Nicolas, clearly disturbed and unsettled by what they had just witnessed. The officers were clearly not prepared for what they had been subjected to and as such it was obvious that they were overwhelmed. Nicolas understood that on the drive back to the office he was not going to be asked for decorating advice. In truth, in terms of other historical murder cases, Nicolas' apartment was like no other, with the possible exception of Jeffrey Dahmer's. However, Dahmer's apartment, while holding the remains of bodies in barrels and fridges, was not decorated in such a macabre fashion as Nicolas' was. Therefore, in terms of such a setting, Nicolas' apartment remains unique.

Back at the police headquarters, the police remained silent; the attitude of the police had changed in dramatic fashion from what it had been prior to the excursion to Nicolas' apartment. It was almost as though the officers wished to dismiss themselves from the case. As far as they were concerned, Nicolas had confessed, all of the evidence had been gathered, and now it was going to be placed in the hands of the prosecuting magistrate on the case. The police seemed to want nothing more to do with the case.

In France, it is the prosecuting magistrate who leads the investigation and as such, the requirement for further police involvement is minimal. It was two days following the gathering of evidence at his apartment that Nicolas was given the opportunity to meet the prosecuting magistrate. His name was Gilbert Thiel, a magistrate from the East of France, who spoke in a strong local accent – an accent which made it nigh-impossible for Nicolas to take him seriously. Gilbert Thiel was at this time famous for having concluded his prosecution of Simone Weber, an infamous female serial killer dubbed 'The She-Devil of Nancy'.

Prosecuting a murder case in France is a long process. The reason for this is that the case is thoroughly investigated, and all evidence and reports are concluded correctly. While the case is being investigated, the suspect is placed in jail to await court and potential sentencing. Therefore, while his case was being concluded, Nicolas was sent to the Fleury-Mérogis prison in the southern suburbs of Paris. This is the largest prison in Europe and can hold up to 5000 prisoners at any given time. The journey from the police headquarters to the prison takes approximately 45 minutes' drive. Nicolas was placed inside of a special bus, which had in it six individual holding cells, all equipped to detain prisoners on the journey to the prison.

Fleury-Mérogis Prison (as at 2016)

The prison itself was separated into five separate units, with each unit housing approximately 1000 inmates. Each unit was named D1, D2, D3 and so forth. It was as though there were five separate sub-prisons within the one prison, with each section being segregated by the category of crime. Nicolas was sent to D4 section, which is for prisoners who have committed their first offence, regardless of the nature of the crime. This section was generally a temporary section of the prison, made up of those who committed mainly white-collar crime and who, until this point in time, had no experience of how the prison service worked. Other prisoners awaiting sentencing would be detained in this section until they had either been given sentencing or had got used to the prison system and could be moved to the section which related to their type of crime. The process of going through the prison system was slow, primarily due to the painstaking process the prosecuting magistrate insists on while the investigation is being completed.

It has been known for this process to take anywhere between two and five years before final sentencing is complete and a prisoner remanded to what would be their ultimate place of custody.

Initially, due to the nature of Nicolas' crime and what was subsequently found in his apartment, strict instructions were given to the prison that Nicolas should not be placed in a cell with another inmate. However, for some reason – perhaps a breakdown in communication – this was not adhered to. Nicolas was placed in a cell with a recovering drug addict. However, as this person was recovering from their addiction, they did nothing but sleep the entirety of the time. After two weeks, though, this error was rectified.

Then came the first visit of Nicolas' parents to the prison. It was an emotional meeting: not only was it difficult for them all to meet in such a surrounding, but it was made still more difficult because, during the entirety of his time in prison, Nicolas had no correspondence with the investigation magistrate, nor from his own lawyer at the time. Because of this, Nicolas had not had the opportunity to speak to his parents and break the news to them, and so they had to find out all of the information from the police. This made this initial meeting between Nicolas and his parents extremely emotional, as naturally they were left bewildered at what had happened, even leading them to question what must have happened to Nicolas in his childhood to make things turn out the way that they had done. Nicolas recalls the entire situation as bleak – having to speak to his parents through a Plexiglass window, in a dirty environment, struggling to make communication seem better than what it was.

From his very first day inside the prison, Nicolas learned how to behave as an inmate. Nicolas studied how the politics of a prison worked, understanding who the main and most revered inmates were, as well as understanding the hierarchy of the prison system. Prisoners who had murdered police officers were at the pinnacle of the system, with prisoners such as child killers, molesters and others such as rapists being the dregs and most detested types of prisoner. There were of course sub-categories to this, and people deemed to be psychotic were tagged as not to be messed with, owing to the unpredictable nature of their mental illnesses. Once the facts of what Nicolas was accused of doing surfaced, combined with various rumours, he was regarded as not to be messed with. There was talk of Nicolas having supernatural powers, where he would be able to place a curse on an unsuspecting inmate, as well as the suspicion of cannibalism which in turn led to inmates believing that Nicolas would 'eat their face' should they cross his path in a manner he did not like.

The saying 'Don't judge a book by its cover' is ever-present in prison: while a person may look sweet and innocent on the outside, underneath that exterior could lie the mentality of a ruthless and sadistic maniac. Therefore, having the aura of a psychopath would indeed give rise to the idea that their actions were often difficult to predict. As a result, people deemed to be psychopaths would generally be left alone and remain 'untouchable'.

Nicolas recalls the 'pros and cons' of being given such a label. The main disadvantage was that people would be intimated by him and that there would therefore be no social interaction between him and the other prisoners. A person of his demeanour could be deemed as being 'bad luck' to be around. However, given Nicolas' isolated upbringing and his general inability to mix socially with others, these were not seen by him in a negative light. If anything, Nicolas did not mind the 'con' side of things, as it was something that he was already accustomed to. Since the 'pro' of the situation meant that he was deemed as a person who was not to be trifled with, ultimately all the 'pros and cons' were all 'pros' as far as Nicolas was concerned, as he was already comfortable in his solitude. The interaction, though, was not that much in any case, with inmates only being allowed out of their cells for one and half hours, twice a day. Therefore, it meant that inmates were locked up for a total of 21 hours a day; the desire to socially interact in those three hours a day outside his cell was not of great importance to Nicolas.

After a month Nicolas was moved to the D1 section of the prison. This was a section that housed inmates who were deemed to be the hardcore criminals within the prison: prisoners who were drug dealers, murderers and bank robbers were all housed within this section of the prison. It was within this section that Nicolas would spend the next three and a half years.

In a prison system that is designed to make inmates walk in the same clockwise direction, so that there is little chance of eye contact and therefore a reduced chance of friction between inmates, everything is designed to maintain a sense of calm as much as possible. However, much as he found in the army, Nicolas realised that despite the instilled sense of order and calm, a hier-archical system still surged within the underbelly of the prison population. Just as in the army, Nicolas had continued to main-tain his large physical appearance by continually working out. As such, the combination of his physical frame with the aura that he carried in relation to his crimes meant that Nicolas was seen as superior by a large amount of the prison population. Not to mention that the vast majority of the criminal population seemed to be, in Nicolas' view, of a lower IQ than that in the outside world, with inmates often being remanded in custody for simple and repeat offences such as not paying a restaurant bill. The smarter and more imposing of the prison inmates would use their size and higher IQ to purposely manipulate the remainder of the popu-lation and as such, gain what could be deemed as 'control' of the inmate population. As Nicolas puts it: 'It was a very large game of chess.' People gained an upper hand either by strength and imposi-tion, or by manipulated politics: not dissimilar to the army or even large social circles on the outside the prison walls.

That was just the politics and manipulation of the inmate population. There were of course outside factors where the same principles applied. At the time, Nicolas' father had used his connections to left-wing radicals from his youth to secure a respected and successful lawyer for his son: Irène Terrel. She was a human rights activist who had represented left-wing terrorists in criminal cases in the past, as well as being a part of the legal team which had represented the infamous 'Carlos the Jackal'. However, after only speaking to Terrel for approximately five minutes, Nicolas realised that she was clueless on how to properly represent him.

Terrel wished to pursue the line of defence on the case from a psychiatric perspective. She insisted that the more Nicolas co-operated with her, the better it would be for the defence's argument. She instructed Nicolas to say that he heard voices in his head, to be very vocal about his crimes – especially to the investigating and prosecuting magistrate – and not to hesitate when it came to displaying symptoms pertaining to mental health. In French law, there is a certain article which states that cases cannot be tried in the same manner as other criminal prosecutions, should there be underlying mental health concerns. In cases such as these, there are two ways in which the crimes can be approached. The first is that the mental state of the accused has been completely abolished, at which point all the charges would then be dropped and the accused would be sent to a mental health facility to spend an undetermined amount of time, being released as and when the ruling psychiatrist determined they were fit and safe to return to the public. However, given that people in cases such as these are more often than not deemed to have permanent mental damage and as such would never be able to re-enter society, this is no different from that of a life sentence, albeit in a different location from a prison, i.e. a unit for the criminally insane.

The second option is when a psychiatrist determines that the accused suffers only from an altered state of mental health, where they acted on an 'altered state of mental capability' but overall was still aware of their actions to a degree, although hampered by this altered state of mental health. This would mean that the charges would not be dropped; however, the accused would have to spend a great deal of time in therapy, while serving a maximum of 15 years in an actual prison.

This gave Nicolas an idea. He did not like the idea of spending the rest of his life in either a prison or a facility for the mentally insane. Therefore, the prospects of receiving a maximum term of 15 years' imprisonment seemed to be far more appealing. As the wait for trial and sentencing was a long process, Nicolas was able to study, in the prison library, the facts regarding having only an altered state of mind. Given that he had studied psychology in university, he had a fundamental grasp of what to look for in his research. Nicolas now accepts that it is actually quite possible that he was then suffering from a state of psychosis or even schizo-phrenia, as these are usually brought on by child abandonment and emotional neglect. However, at the time it was his mission to research this to the best of his ability, so that he would be able to convince the psychiatrist who was employed on behalf of the prosecution that he was, in fact, suffering from an altered mental state while committing his crimes and, therefore, had diminished responsibility for them.

Nicolas researched the symptoms as well as he could. He read every book that he found on the subject. He learned that the onset of the relevant symptoms developed primarily in the teenage years. What is more, he learned that it was not enough just to state that he only heard voices: he would also have to state that he heard the voices in his head in 'stereo', as a person who claims to hear voices in one ear only is deemed to be faking the symptoms.

Nicolas knew that he would have to behave himself while he was in jail: his back was against the wall and he was now in survival mode. He had accepted that he was not going to evade punishment. However, he could use his intellect and persuasive abilities to get himself the least amount of years in terms of punishment, by convincing the prosecution that he had acted with diminished responsibility. Nicolas was about to play the most important chess game of his life!

ELEVEN

JUDGEMENT

Prison, Trial and Sentencing

DARWINISM IS THE theory of biological evolution developed by English naturalist Charles Darwin in the 19th century. It states that all species of organisms arose and developed through a natural process where different individuals within the groups of organisms were better adapted to their environment and reproduced in greater numbers.

Humans are particularly good at manipulating this process by consciously adapting to their surroundings in modern life. A person may, or may not, have the ability to adapt in order to survive, physically, emotionally and even mentally. Those who recognise the need to adapt, and are able to do so, not only survive their situation or predicament, but also flourish as a result of their adaptation abilities.

As with all organisms, there are certain types who do not display adaptability to an ever-changing environment. In human terms, it is extremely rare that a person without the ability to adapt will ever find themselves in a position of prominence, or even able to move from the bottom levels of a social, political, or even professional standings. The person without adaptability will find themselves left behind by their 'evolutionary' superiors.

Some people find that their evolutionary instincts become engaged when they are faced with the prospect of physical or even mental danger. However, it is the people who use their intelligence to foresee the potential of what is to come, that can recognise that they are going to have to adapt in order to not only survive, but minimise the potential for negative prospects going forward. It is a case of learning from mistakes that have been made, all the while ensuring that the consequences for all those mistakes result in the least amount of detriment to their own lives. They adapt to survive in the best way that they can.

As previously stated, the wait for a trial in France can be a lengthy, drawn-out process. In Nicolas' case, this process was lengthened even further because the prosecuting magistrate undertook such a thorough investigation. In his time awaiting trial, while remaining in prison, Nicolas was sent to work in the gym area of the prison, a role which he was happy to take on as it resulted in him being allowed more time out of his cell. (Without this work, he would have had to remain in his cell for 21 hours a day.)

In the gym area, Nicolas was recognised by a tall man, who had seen Nicolas up to three times a day in the Pigalle district of Paris. Each day, on leaving and returning to his apartment, Nicolas would walk past a nearby bar, but what he did not know was that this bar was a favourite meeting spot for Parisian gangsters; as such, the gangsters would be on the lookout for any signs of police or even rival gang members outside the bar. The tall man asked Nicolas if he was part of any of the local Pigalle district gangs. Nicolas replied that he was not and, instead, went on to explain his case to the man. The man himself was a professional burglar, who over time, would give Nicolas hints and tips on how to gain access into buildings and such.

Prison was repetitive and quite often mundane. Even though the threat of trial loomed, it was important to find things to do that passed the time. The opportunity of working in the gym made Nicolas' life that little bit easier, especially as this gave him the ability to put any people he wanted onto the prison gym lists. Nicolas would place the names of the old-timer gangsters on the lists, not so that they could work out in the gym, but more that they had a place to relax outside their cells and play cards. This gesture made Nicolas favourable in their eyes.

It was from these interactions that Nicolas was able to see for himself the politics of prison life. There were a lot of people on the prison block that were professionals, 'career criminals', primarily involved with the trafficking and sale of drugs. While people of different ethnicities seemed to stick to their own groups inside prison, this rule appeared to be broken for criminals in the drug trade, where there was some sort of a cross-over. Although Nicolas was not interested in drugs, whether selling or using, he was able to see that the politics were that while a person should primarily be seen to be congregating with people of their own ethnicity, it was perfectly acceptable to be seen to be doing business with other ethnicities. What was a contradiction, however, was that a 'skinhead' with racist views, say, was not frowned upon by his own kind for doing business with people from a hated ethnic group. This is similar to the prison scene in the movie *American History X*, where a person who identifies as a Nazi can be seen doing drug business with people from a minority ethnic group, completely contradicting the Nazis' own core principles. Nicolas found the environment to be strange; however, he put it down to people just wanting to earn extra money and pass the time, despite it being a strange 'political' situation.

Nicolas was spending a lot of his time preparing and researching for his case and the forthcoming trial. Other than his preparation work, there was very little to do to pass the time. However, a surprising change in his mail correspondence would become the fundamental cornerstone of his future activities.

Nicolas received a letter, which was adorned with a return address in Tampa, in the US state of Florida. The writer had received Nicolas' prison address from the creators of the fanzine *Boiled Angels*. The fanzine, which Nicolas had previously read and used to correspond with other readers, had brought out an issue featuring Nicolas and the murder for which he was being sent to trial. Nicolas responded to the letter and in turn he began to receive more letters from people interested in not only the fanzine, but Nicolas' case as well. The letters that Nicolas began to receive in prison were from a variety of different people, people from all walks of life, including true crime collectors, housewives, doctors and even people from law enforcement.

In one of the letters, Nicolas was asked if he had produced any art at all, as the person in question was a collector of art pertaining to true crime and the crime's perpetrators. In response, Nicolas sent them a tracing of the outline of his hand. Following on from this, Nicolas was sent pictures and postcards of graveyards, as well as various stamps. Nicolas liked receiving these things, as it helped him to pass the time while in prison, awaiting his trial.

One correspondent then proceeded to ask if Nicolas had produced any paintings, which at that time he had not. It did, however, give him the idea to try and give painting a try, so he decided to acquire some art supplies. Nicolas began by painting a picture of Highgate cemetery, in London, which was featured on one of the postcards that he had received as 'fan' mail. He decided to try to replicate the postcard as best he could. By his own admission, his earliest paintings were not the best in terms of quality, however, he enjoyed getting the opportunity to be creative. Further to this, the people he sent the paintings to seemed to be thrilled merely at the fact of receiving art from him.

This seems to have spurred Nicolas on to try and develop his art skills. Among the mail that he received while in prison was a tattoo magazine, which for some reason featured a photograph of notorious cult leader Charles Manson. This was the now-famous mugshot which depicts Manson as having 'crazy eyes'. Nicolas decided that he was going to replicate this photo as a painting, only he wished to put his own stamp on it. Nicolas chose to use different colours for his painting: he used black shades of paint, along with a titanium-white colour to create a 'ghost-face' appearance, and added a blood-red background to the painting, all serving to make the central portrait stand out further still. In time this would become what Nicolas now describes as his signature painting style: a style that would later be evident throughout a vast majority of his works, serving as a kind of trademark.

His artwork began to become well known in the Tampa area of Florida and even caught the attention of people associated with local death metal bands such as Cannibal Corpse (who also featured in the Jim Carrey movie *Ace Ventura*) and Morbid Angel. In return for his artwork, the people associated with these bands would send Nicolas autographed pictures of the bands, which Nicolas thought was really quite cool.

Nicolas' artwork, as well as news of his crimes, had started to gain the attention of people all over America, as well as other countries in Europe. As a result, he began to receive more mail in prison, as well as more requests for his artwork.

Nicolas' painting was displayed at an expo in New Orleans by true crime collector Rick Staton, known for his dealings as the 'middle man' selling murder memorabilia to famous celebrities such as Johnny Depp, Leonardo DiCaprio and Iggy Pop, among others. Staton went on to purchase the now-famous painting of serial killer John Wayne Gacy, in which Gacy had painted himself as 'Pogo the Clown'. Staton would begin what became known as 'Murderabilia', where he obtained items related to true crime for his collection. This was not as popular at the time as it is today. However, the demand for artwork and crime memorabilia seemed to be taking off as a vibrant new trend, a trend which to this day remains strong. In truth, it could be said that people such as Rick Staton started this trend, which others would soon follow and popularise. Prior to this, John Wayne Gacy would do commissioned paintings from his cell on death row for a low price – in the region of $200. Now, however, due to the popularity of the genre, Gacy's paintings have been known to sell for anywhere between $2000 and $12,000. Collecting material relating to true crime cases was boosted in popularity by people such as Arthur Rosenblatt, who became known as having the *crème de la crème* of true crime memorabilia, including, at one point, Ted Bundy's Volkswagen 'Bug' in his collection.

One day, Nicolas received another letter with the return postal address of a prison in California. To his complete surprise, the letter was from a person called Patrick Kearney. Kearney was known first as the 'Freeway Killer' and later the 'Trash Bag Killer' after he was convicted of killing over 30 people in the 1970s and having dismembered the bodies and disposed of the remains in rubbish bags (hence the name). The letter was written to Nicolas in French. To his surprise, Nicolas discovered that Kearney, as well as being infamous for his own killings, had shared cells in close proximity to both Charles Manson and serial killer Ed Kemper. This gave Nicolas the idea to begin writing to other serial killers, such as Richard Ramirez, as well as a vast number of others. In addition to this, Nicolas received mail from apparently 'like-minded' people, which confirmed to him that people emulate those they admire.

While Nicolas developed his art skills and continued to correspond with people from what seemed to be all over the world, his case continued to draw closer to his trial date. The prosecution was slowly building up their case against Nicolas. A second search of his apartment was ordered by the prosecuting magistrate; this time, though, the search was focused on what books and posters Nicolas had collected, as the magistrate was trying to build a mental landscape of Nicolas' persona, focussing primarily on the 'Vampire' aspect.

At the same time, the prosecution magistrate Thiel was making every effort to connect Nicolas to a string of other murders. These were the murders which Nicolas' interrogating officer had asked him about and which had been coincidentally similar in vein to Nicolas' dreams about killing people. However, as there was a lack of physical evidence – to be specific, there was a lack of a murder weapon – the prosecution were not able to proceed with adding these crimes to his case. Nicolas recalls:

'From what I heard, there were another two cases, and I don't know, maybe they eventually found the real culprit.'

The way Magistrate Thiel conducted his prosecution cases was held in high regard, so when a series of nail bombs were detonated in Paris, he was included as part of the Anti-Terrorism Unit. As such he was instructed to drop all of his other cases to focus entirely on the new division that he was assigned to. He did so, with two exceptions. At the time there was a serial killer active in Paris, dubbed 'The Beast of the Bastille' by the media, who had murdered about seven or eight women in Paris by slitting their throats with a knife. The case was labelled by the police as the 'SK1' case at the time magistrate Thiel was assigned to the case. This was one of the two cases that Thiel did not hand over to another magistrate; the other was Nicolas' case.

As part of the prosecution, Nicolas was continually questioned and interrogated by the magistrate, though such questioning was not done at the prison. In fact, in order for Thiel to question Nicolas, he would be taken from the prison and brought back to the *Brigade Criminelle*. This time, however, Thiel was not located at the top of the building where Nicolas was initially taken to after his arrest. Thiel's new offices were now in the newly formed Anti-Terrorist Unit, which was under even tighter security restrictions, given the nature of the department.

When Nicolas was brought to Thiel's office, he could see all the files on his desk pertaining not only to his own case, and the other cases to which Thiel had been trying to connect him to, but also the anti-terrorism and the SK1 cases. Further to speaking to Thiel, Nicolas was required to talk to up to ten experts for the prosecution, comprising psychiatrists, psychologists, cognitive behaviour experts and other professionals of a similar ilk. Nicolas was asked to draw pictures for the experts, which he did. Each time he would draw stick men for them and give the stick men massive eyes, except that none of the eyes would ever have any pupils in them. Further to this, Nicolas was asked to look at art, such as ink blots and asked what he could see in the ink blots. Each and every one of Nicolas' replies was that he saw human bones. For example, for one ink blot Nicolas would state that the image resembled a leg bone, then the next one he would say that the blot looked like a mandible bone from the jawline, and so forth. In truth, Nicolas did not see any bones at all in the ink blots, but he found that saying that he did not only confused the expert opinions, but helped his own case.

Nicolas was made to undergo analysis by the experts for up to a year. In that time, extensive tests were undertaken, all of which Nicolas had prepared himself for by his research in the prison library. By law, he was given access to all of the files regarding his case, and in one of the files that he kept, an expert was quoted as saying (loosely translated from French):

'This is a young man, who as a child had some hypnagogic experiences following the death of his grandfather. He would develop an interest in witchcraft, magic, Satan and embalming. Later as a young adult he would collect movies related to horror, S&M and autopsies. This progressed to the development of conditions of occult scenarios which were accomplished by megalomania, where he was chosen by the Devil to be his weapon and begin his reign here on earth. These beliefs and practices expanded into the world of physical death, by beginning a career in embalming [which was false; Nicolas was a morgue technician] where he would dissect and consume bits of bodies in what would be compared to a reverse connotation of the ritualistic communion of Christ. By eating flesh and ritualised gore, he would get closer to the demons that he worshipped.'

Nicolas discovered that psychology was just another belief system with certain patterns which we, as people, are meant to follow. Should a person stray outside these patterns, then the experts tend to be clueless as to why. If a person follows a pattern, then it can be assumed that they can be cured. Therefore, should a person not be following any distinguishable patterns, then the experts would believe that a cure for the behaviour is not possible. Nicolas understood that if he did not follow any form of a pattern, then it would be taken as a sign that he would not be able to be cured: as such, there was little probability of a life beyond prison walls, or at any rate hospital walls. He decided that he would play the game and give the experts a pattern to distinguish and identify, so that despite having to face the consequences of jail, it would not be forever.

The date set for Nicolas' trial was the 8th of May, 1997. He had been held in prison for over two and half years and in that time he had prepared himself as best he could. Now with such a short time to go, it was time to begin mentally preparing for the trial. During this time Nicolas had been speaking to a fellow inmate, who was a member of the 'Bandidos' motorcycle gang. Nicolas noticed a tattoo on the gang member's arm. It was the occult symbol for 'Lucifuge Rofocale', who according to the *Grande Grimoire* is the demon in charge of Hell's government, by order of the Devil. Nicolas knew immediately by looking at the tattoo that this man had made a pact with the Devil. Initially, Nicolas did not say anything to the gang member about the tattoo, as he chose to get to know the man a little before doing so. However, as his trial was approaching, Nicolas decided to ask about the man's tattoo. The gang member stated that while he did not know the origins of the source of the tattoo, he had previously shared a cell with a gypsy while in another prison, and this cell mate had performed a black magic ritual with the gang member as means as to try and hope for a lesser prison sentence. Seemingly, it had worked and he was given a lesser sentence. (When Nicolas met him, he was imprisoned for a different crime.)

Image of Lucifuge Rofocale, from the Grande Grimoire

Nicolas knew of the demon Lucifuge Rofocale from his extensive occult interest and beliefs over the years. Therefore, he decided that he would create a pact with the demon himself, as means for a lesser sentence. On 30th April 1997 – *Walpurgisnacht*, a Catholic saint's day now better known as the 'Witches' Sabbath' – just over one week before his trial was set to commence, Nicolas made his pact with the demon. He wrote his pact on a piece of paper, which said 'By the blood in my veins, I promise to honour and serve the Prince of Darkness until the day that I die. I seal the pact in my own blood.'

Nicolas' pact

Nicolas took a blade from a BIC disposable razor and carved the symbol of the demon into his own bicep, then smeared the blood from the bicep on the previously written pact. Nicolas recalls feeling a rush of energy surging throughout his body after doing so.

The morning of the trial, May 8th, he was transferred to the *Cour d'Assise* (High Court) in Paris, where the trial was to take place. At the beginning of the trial, the family of the victim had petitioned the courts to run the trial as a *Huis Clos*, in other words with a closed-door policy and media blackout to the public and media, as they did not wish to have their family member's exploits on websites such as Minitel exposed to the public. The prosecution, however, disagreed, as they wished for all aspects to be made public as a way of exposing the dangers of certain subcultures, such as Minitel and the occult. What was decided in the end was a half-and-half policy, in which certain aspects of the crime would be allowed to be exposed and other aspects hidden from public and media attention.

The judge who presided over the trial was called Bruno Waechter. Inside the courtroom, to Nicolas' right, was the audience which was allowed in the courtroom at periodic moments; to his left was the jury for the trial. Each party to the proceedings, that is, the defence and the prosecution, were allowed to exchange three jurors of their choice. The defence team seemed to be happy with each of the jurors, with the exception of one: a woman who seemed to be thrilled at the prospect of being on the jury, who was wearing a Christian cross around her neck. The defence had the elated woman exchanged. This turned out to be a smart move, as the woman had apparently wanted to be on the jury as a way of punishing a so-called 'occult crime'.

The defence team had decided to enter a plea of guilty, but with diminished responsibility owing to temporary mental incapacity. It was the prosecution who were allowed to proceed first.

In Nicolas' opinion, the trial started badly for him and the defence team. Initially, the autopsy reports were discussed, as well as testimony from a police officer by the name of Garcin, who was an experienced officer. Garcin went on to describe the crime scene, as well as Nicolas' apartment, giving graphic details of the posters on the walls, the décor of human bones and skulls, as well as describing the video tapes and weapons that were discovered. The jury seemed horrified by this, an impression that was bolstered further by enlarged photographs of both the crime scene and Nicolas' apartment.

It was not a good beginning for Nicolas and the defence team, a notion made worse by the depiction of Nicolas by the experienced police officer, who in addition to relaying his horror at what he had discovered at Nicolas' apartment, also blackened Nicolas' image by describing the look in Nicolas' eyes and drawing comparisons with Thierry Paulin, a French serial killer who had killed up to 21 people. Further to this, testimony was given for the prosecution by people that had known Nicolas in the past. The members of the Human Resources department of St Joseph's Hospital had spoken to the court; however, in order to avoid scandal and embarrassment to the hospital, any charges for the theft of the blood bags and the human flesh had already been dropped. The Human Resources officials stated that Nicolas was never left alone in the morgue, which was a lie. However, should they have admitted this, it would have led to an investigation into the hospital, as it was against hospital protocol and law for someone to be alone in the morgue. The fact that the hospital had made such an error turned out to be favourable for the defence team. (It should be noted that cannibalism is not actually illegal in France. However, the theft of the flesh and the bags of blood would have been. On the other hand, admitting that theft had taken place would have been detrimental to the hospital's reputation.)

Further testimony for the prosecution was given by more people that Nicolas knew. These ranged from former classmates, who stated to the court that in the past Nicolas had threatened to kill them, to people from the heavy metal scene. These witnesses, who were supposed to have been his friends, stated that he was leading a double life and that, had they been fully aware of his crimes, then they would have certainly reported him to the relevant authorities. Even his own uncle – the same uncle Nicolas had stayed with following his grandfather's death and prior to his family's relocation to Portugal; the same uncle who had acquired the illegal copy of *PHOTO* magazine which reproduced photographs of the victim of Japanese student Issei Sagawa – testified that he thought Nicolas was a strange child, capable of extreme measures. The prosecution even went as far as to take testimony from the tattoo artist who had done the words 'Serial' and 'Killer' on each of Nicolas' arms. This man stated that he did not wish to put the tattoos on Nicolas but felt as though he was powerless to refuse. He said that Nicolas deserved to have these words emblazoned on him as he looked and acted like a serial killer would, in his opinion. Even the lawyer for the prosecution made reference to the fact that, in the prosecution's opinion, Nicolas had 'Death Eyes'.

Nicolas' lawyer advised him to be as vocal as he possibly could be throughout the trial and in particular to react verbally to witness testimony for the duration of the trial. If Nicolas were to remain silent during the testimonies, it could have been seen by the jury as a hostile attitude and could as a result lead them to believe that he was deserving of a lifetime in prison. Nicolas knew that when the experts were talking about him, the jury would be looking in his direction. Therefore, Nicolas played up to whatever the experts were saying, even going as far as sit there with his mouth open, gazing forward in a blank fashion as his personality or disorders were being discussed – almost to be seen as 'out of his mind', in a manner of speaking. Nicolas was playing his role to the letter. He was, though, in a fight for his eventual freedom and his life and, as such, was doing all that he could to adapt to his surroundings so that he could survive.

Of the six experts who testified as to the level of Nicolas' state of mind, four of them returned the professional opinion that, although hampered by his mental issues, he was not entirely without blame for his actions. He was suffering from a degree of borderline psychosis and as such, he did not belong in a facility for the mentally impaired. He was stated to have suffered from a mental disorder and therefore not entirely responsible for his actions; in truth, just a diminished responsibility. The remaining two experts both stated that Nicolas should be remanded to a psychiatric hospital indefinitely, as they felt that his mental condition was entirely to blame for his actions.

Following all of the testimonies of both the public and of the experts, it was time for the closing statements to be given. A lawyer representing the victim's family was allowed to speak first. The lawyer for the family stated that it was their opinion that Nicolas was manipulative, impulsive, ego-centred and that they believed that should Nicolas be given the opportunity in the future, he would almost certainly kill again, since all his intelligence was focused on gathering weapons and drawing inspiration from an evil source.

The team for the prosecution seemed to echo this lawyer's sentiments, their statement comparing Nicolas to a major serial killer. Throughout the trial, they had tried to connect Nicolas to other cases and continued to do so even in their closing statement, without any proof. In the second part of the closing statement, the audience and the media were removed from the room and it was here that the prosecution made reference to the fact that despite the hospital not wishing to press charges, Nicolas was considered to be a cannibal and a vampire and was extremely dangerous. They tried to sway the jury to not only sentence him for the murder, but also to sentence him for what he was perceived to be. The implication was that the only reason that any possible surviving victims of Nicolas' crimes had not come forward to the police with complaints was that they did not wish to be shamed for having been on the S&M section of the Minitel forums.

During the final summations of the prosecution, a girl in the room waved at Nicolas. Nicolas was confused, unsure whether it was him that the girl was waving at or not. It *was* Nicolas whose attention the girl was trying to get, and it transpired that one of the jurors had noticed this happening. However, rather than draw anyone's attention to the girl, the juror merely laughed at the situation. It was through this that Nicolas was able to note that half of the jury were not really paying attention to the lawyer for the prosecution.

The next day, it was the turn of Nicolas' lawyer Irène Terrel to make her closing statements. Nicolas was not aware of what her strategy was going to be and as such, was surprised at her approach to this. As a coincidence, the Cannes Film Festival was only a few days away from opening that year in France. This year there was an array of controversial films that would be presented at the festival: *Funny Games* and *Assassin*, along with the Johnny Depp film *The Brave*, which is essentially a fictional depiction of a snuff film. Nicolas' lawyer stated that they lived in a society that depicts violence in everyday life, even as far as the popular and notable Cannes Film Festival, where violence is seen as a form of entertainment. Therefore, a person who is deemed to have a strong personality disorder would be heavily influenced by the portrayals of violence in film and the media, affecting their perceptions of reality. Nicolas did not think that the jury was really listening to his lawyer, as it was common practice for any lawyers connected to the radical left to find a means of something else to blame for a person's actions. It was only when Terrel mentioned Satanic heavy metal, citing it as an influence, that the jury seemed to take note and were in agreement.

Finally, it was Nicolas' turn to speak. In doing so, he cemented what his lawyer had stated by repeating her sentiments. He stated that when he was released he was going to devote his life to becoming the best citizen that he possibly could, as well as never allowing himself to be influenced by evil horror movies or Satanic heavy metal ever again. He vowed to never attend heavy metal concerts again and, further to this, his days of frequenting graveyards were behind him. The jury, in response, seemed to nod at Nicolas and even went as far as to smile at him. Nicolas was playing the role as best he could and, in his own words, 'he should have received an Oscar that day' for his performance in the courtroom.

As the jury deliberated as to their verdict, Nicolas was remanded to the holding cells of the court. The security officers of the court are hired professionals who, due to the fact that anything that is said could be used in evidence, are instructed not to speak or engage with the defendants under any circumstances. However, when one of the two officers that escorted Nicolas to the waiting cells left and it was just the other officer and Nicolas in the room, he turned to Nicolas and asked, 'What does it taste like?' – referring to human flesh. Nicolas just looked at the officer for a moment, smirked at him and didn't answer.

It took the jury only six hours to deliberate their verdict. As Nicolas had entered a plea of guilty, but by diminished responsibility, the verdict was not to determine guilt, but more to establish the level of responsibility that he had in relation to his crimes. Therefore, a verdict of guilty was a given. After the six hours had passed and everyone had congregated into the courtroom, the jury delivered their verdict of guilty, by reason of diminished responsibility. The sentence that the jury wished to impose was that Nicolas was to serve a term of no more than 12 years in prison. It was the verdict that Nicolas was hoping for. The family of the victim was not happy with the verdict and subsequent sentence of 12 years' imprisonment. However, in French Law at the time there was no means for the family to appeal the sentence.

Nicolas had got what he wanted: his pact with Lucifuge Rofocale had worked.

Eventually, Nicolas would be sent to the Maison Centrale de Poissy Maximum security prison in Paris to conclude the remainder of his sentence. He had already served three years awaiting trial and calculated that, with good behaviour, he would be eligible for release in just four years' time. Nicolas had not got away with murder, but if there was ever an outcome that could be deemed as 'the next best thing', then this was it.

This was not the end for Nicolas Claux. This was to be just another chapter in a life that could be deemed extraordinary at the very least. A life that would continue to be filled with extraordinary correspondence with an array of serial killers, a life dealing with memorabilia from vast amounts of crime scenes, a life filled with the art steeped in cannibalistic and murderous stylings – and, most intriguingly of all, a life which continued to be contained within the interiors of a morgue.

INTERVIEW WITH NICOLAS CLAUX

THIS BOOK COULD not be concluded without a selection from the interviews that I have conducted with Nicolas. Therefore, it was decided that a small Q & A section would be a fitting way to draw a close to the final chapter of this book. We already have a detailed and exclusive insight as to the story of Nicolas Claux; however, as an added insight, here is one such discussion.

B K Jackson – 1) The first thing that I have to ask, which I think people will be interested to know, is whether or not you have any remorse?
Nicolas – Yes and no. I try not to linger on things, so I guess... not really...

2) Looking back then, is there anything that you would have changed?
Well, I always wanted to be a chemist, as being a chemist would have given me access to bio-weapons, so I think you can see where this is headed. If I had have become a chemist, things would have turned out very differently. If you had asked me that question while I was still in jail, then I guess the answer that I would have given would have been very different from now. But looking at my life now, I have a good life and I am happy, I have an amazing girlfriend, I get to enjoy things.

Everything that I have done in life has brought me to where I am today and I am happy, so no…I wouldn't change anything.

3) *What are people's reactions to you today? When people find out who you are, how do you get treated?*

It depends. For example, if I were to visit a goth club in France, or something similar, people would tend to whisper, talk behind my back, look down when I walk past them, or even make eye contact. Then after a while, I will get a message from the owner of the goth club asking me not to come back, as it gives the goth club a bad name.

Then take, for example, a place like Sweden. Within five minutes of being there, I am asked by people to have selfies taken with them, they want autographs, even asking if they can buy me a beer. So, what does this tell me? French people suck! Especially French journalists, who will offer you nothing other than Champagne so that a little bit of alcohol loosens the tongue, so that they can get a story out of you. It makes me naturally suspicious. Thankfully though, it is a new generation of people these days, so it gets better, and with more respect.

4) *Apart from psychiatrists' mental health diagnosis, how do you feel that your mental health is affected today? How do you overcome it?*

Well, these days I am a lot more social. In the past, I didn't fit in as much. Whereas now I have found a community (the true crime community) that I do fit in with. Because it is done with respect and in turn I respect those people. If I have anyone to thank for my mental health it is them. I have noticed that it has a lot to do with my environment. When I was a kid I didn't have this type of environment and that make it difficult. These days I am surrounded by a good environment, so my mental health is good. Of course, when I lost my dream job in the morgue recently, I was depressed, but because of who I have around me I was able to react in a different way. The penal system, in truth, did not do shit for my mental health at all. It is my own environment that helped the most.

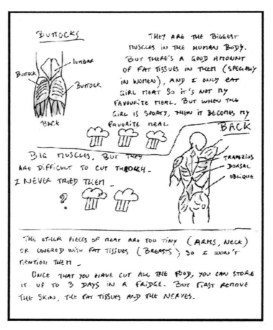

A page from Nicolas' book of recipes

5) *Does the taste of human flesh taste different from other parts of the human body? Or example, ribs and legs?*

Yes, definitely. For example, the ribs have meat which has more fibres, which makes the meat less tender than other parts of the body. The legs have far more tender meat and that makes it easier to eat. It is not just different parts of the body that taste different, it is also other factors like their diet and even their ethnicity that has an impact. For example, a person who was on the Captain Cook expedition in the 1700s [said that on islands] where they engaged in cannibalism, it was noted that people who were islanders seemed to taste sweet, black people tasted salty and Europeans tasted like shit. I haven't eaten the flesh of someone from America, but I imagine that with the fast-food industry it is not going to make them taste nice. Although if any Americans wish to donate their meat for 'science' purposes, they know where to find me.

6) *What prevents you from killing today?*
Paperwork... It is a pain in the arse, unnecessary and a complete pain. Having to sign that many documents just isn't worth it.

7) *Obviously we are going to discuss your correspondence with serial killers such as Richard Ramirez, David Berkowitz and Ian Brady in the next book, amongst many, many others, but from a killer's point of view, who do you feel that you relate to the most?*
Perhaps 'relate' isn't the right word, but in Austria, there was a killer called Jack Unterweger, who in the '70s was convicted of murder and sentenced to 20 years in prison. While in prison he taught himself to read and then wrote a book. The intellectual elite thought this was amazing and that he was reformed, making him a prize example of their reformation process. Unterweger was then given the job of a journalist who was then sent to America to stay in the Cecil Hotel that Richard Ramirez had been staying at, to write about crime in Los Angeles. During that time Unterweger began another killing spree by killing sex workers, as well as more murders in Europe. After finally being tracked down and caught, he killed himself in his prison cell. Then you take someone like me, who was convicted of murder and people thought that there was no way back for me because of the cannibalism, etc. But yet here I am, I publish books on true crime, I do paintings and also create marvellous sex toys for sale, as well as memorabilia from Armin Meiwes' house, all for sale on my site www.serialpleasures.com. So it's not that I

relate to Unterweger, but it shows me that no one is predictable, and that the intellectuals actually don't know shit.

8) *I have read your book called* The Cannibal Cookbook *in which you have human meat recipes from all over the world. I found it to be dark, informative and even laced with dark humour. Is there any message that you also hoped to get across with this book?*
The only thing that I wanted to convey with the book is that anything is possible.

9) *Do you feel that Death and, in particular, your relationship with 'The Lady in White' still follows you to this day?*
Yes, definitely. I still have a strong relationship with death. Outside of prison and the morgues I still surround myself with skulls and bones, as well as still visiting graveyards. The only difference is that I don't fear death or the Lady in White the same way other people do. It is like all good books: all books have a final chapter, as do all people. The only thing is that when it is my own final chapter and when it happens, it is going to be met with grandiose and panache. Panache is important. It will happen, but just 'Not today, Satan!'

10) *Finally, we have spoken in great detail about your life, but to all of the readers in this book, is there a final message, or even final words, that you would like to say?*
Just to believe in your own *Dharma*. If there is something that is meant for you, then do it. Believe in it, do it for yourself, not for others. Do not fear judgement of any kind as no one has the right to judge you. Not even your own gods. If your gods are there to judge you, then your gods are weak. Whatever it is that you are meant to do in life, do it to the best of your ability, whether it be a lawyer or whatever it is, believe in yourself. There is one exception and that is not to harm animals or

children. If that is your *Dharma* to do these things, then your *Dharma* is weak, so find another.

Believe in yourself, believe in your *Dharma* and to your inner flame. Do what it is that you are meant to do.

CLOSING WORDS

THERE ARE MANY ways that a person can look at true crime, or indeed any form of a story that has happened in real life. As with everything in life, there are aspects that will be seen in a different light in the views of one person to another.

People will always have a difference of opinion with regards to true crime perpetrators. Some may think that a death penalty or even life imprisonment is suitable, whereas other people will believe that whatever sentence that has been carried out is adequate. What I feel can be agreed is that true crime, to this day, is fascinating, whether it be for historical reference or entertainment in terms of movies based on people like Ted Bundy, who has had numerous films made about his life and exploits. Either way, the interest in the subject has always been there and will probably always be there in one format or another.

The purpose of this book has been not to glorify or even condemn the life of Nicolas Claux. I have my own opinions on the matter, but they are only that, my opinions. The purpose of this book has been to tell the story of his life in a chronological sequence, taking his tales from childhood up until the point of his incarceration. There are very few published books that have been penned from the point of view of the perpetrator in question, as the vast majority of the books written on these subjects tend to be written from the point of view of witnesses to a childhood, authorities that make the arrests, the lawyers that both defend and prosecute the individuals, and the friends and family of the victims themselves. This has been Nicolas' story, from his own words, as the details as they unfolded in his mind. It is up to you to make up your own mind on the subject.

What I will say is that I am grateful to have been let into Nicolas' world, to be given the opportunity to tell his story. I have spent countless hours speaking to Nicolas about his life, and even though this book is packed full with events from his life, I can safely say that there is a lot more to come. From here we will be collaborating again to tell the story of the time that he spent in prison, to go into great detail about his correspondence with notorious serial killers like Richard Ramirez, Ian Brady, Arthur Shawcross (the 'Genesee River Killer'), David Berkowitz (the 'Son of Sam' killer), and even famed killers such as Peter Sutcliffe, as well as discussing items from people such as Aileen Wuornos, the 'Rotenburg Cannibal' Armin Meiwes and the famed cannibal Issei Sagawa. Nicolas' correspondents amount to over 30 well-known serial killers, not to mention the 'murder art' dealings, as well as the additional 15 years that Nicolas spent working in morgues after his release.

What I can say is that if you found this book to be captivating, then you are going to be in for an extensive journey through the mental psyche with the next book.

Thank you to Nicolas for taking the countless hours speaking to me to make this book possible, and thank you to everyone who has an interest in true crime for making the subject interesting enough for me to deem it necessary to write about it. I look forward to taking the next journey into the darkness with each and every one of you.

B K Jackson

THANK YOU

WHILE I HAVE, until this point, been primarily a fiction writer, I simply could not turn down the opportunity to write about one of my favourite subjects, true crime.

Therefore, the very first person that I have to thank in all of this is, of course, Nicolas himself. He very selflessly gave up his time to share with me his unique story. While not knowing me prior to the time we spent writing, he trusted me enough to portray the story in a manner that would remain true to the intimate details of his life. For this I am eternally grateful.

As always, I could not have done any of this without the help and support of those around me. To my dad, Keith, who, despite thinking that I am crazy, never stops giving his full and devoted support to anything that I do that he knows I take enjoyment and fulfilment in.

To Saya, who still thinks that I am famous, because I have written a few books, with the hope that, one day, one of them gets turned into a movie!

To the people that I work with, Neil, Megan and Sophie, who each week cannot wait for updates on what I am writing and, without realising it, have made the weekly debriefing of my writing exploits a further channel in which to tell more intricate stories.

To Kelly, who despite not fully understanding my mind in terms of where the next crazy idea is going to come from, never wanes in her support and pride at what I am doing. As stated in my previous book, Kelly has undertaken some of the cooking duties at home, so that I am free to write as often as I can. Since my last book, Kelly has actually made three meals that have tasted good, and while she is full of self-pride at this revelation, I have no option but to point out to her that I have written as many books in a year as she has good meals prepared! Despite your culinary endeavours, I love you to the stars and back, regardless of what we have for dinner.

As always, to my dearly departed mum, Lynda. This all stemmed from our mutual love of sharing good books. I love and miss you every single day and I hope that I am making you proud with what I am doing, as I am proud to have had such a wonderful mother.

Finally, to all of you who read my books and make all of this possible. I could not do it without all of you! So thank you!

I love each and every one of you.

B K Jackson